Roberto Suro

REMEMBERING THE AMERICAN DREAM

HISPANIC IMMIGRATION AND NATIONAL POLICY

A Twentieth Century Fund Paper

1994 ◆ The Twentieth Century Fund Press ◆ New York

The Twentieth Century Fund sponsors and supervises timely analyses of economic policy, foreign affairs, and domestic political issues. Not-for-profit and nonpartisan, the Fund was founded in 1919 and endowed by Edward A. Filene.

Library of Congress Cataloging-in-Publication Data

Suro, Roberto.
    Remembering the American dream / Roberto Suro.
        p.   cm.
    "A Twentieth Century Fund paper."
    Includes index.
    ISBN 0–87078–194–4 : $9.95
    1. Hispanic Americans—Government policy.   2. United States—Emigration and immigration—Government policy.   I. Twentieth Century Fund.   II. Title.
E184.S75S85   1994
325'.28'0973—dc20   94–3744
                                                                                        CIP

Cover Design, Illustration, and Graphics: Claude Goodwin
Manufactured in the United States of America.
Copyright © 1994 by the Twentieth Century Fund, Inc.

FOREWORD

Through the middle years of the twentieth century, Americans became quite comfortable with the idea that they were part of "a nation of immigrants." Perhaps their contentment was largely a result of the fact that during this period restrictive immigration policies reduced newcomers to a trickle. The last great waves of families from Eastern and Southern Europe had been present long enough and their children were sufficiently Americanized for a sense of stability to take hold across the nation. Indeed, the major movement of peoples that demanded attention and shaped the national agenda involved the migration of black Americans from the fields of the South to the cities of the North.

Like so much of the recent past, however, that time now seems remarkably remote and uncomplicated. Over the past generation, immigration has surged again, reaching levels not seen since the turn of the century. And the turmoil that accompanies such change—this time involving most notably a large increase in new immigrants from Latin America—parallels that of earlier periods of upheaval. The truth is that, in terms of the quantity and ethnic origins of its new residents, the United States is still a work in progress.

For all the limits and exceptions to the rule, the United States remains, in fact, unique in its continuing willingness to accept significant waves of very diverse immigrants. Therefore, surges in immigration and alterations in its sources mean that Americans continue to adapt to an element of change that exceeds that of any other nation. At any given moment, the children of previous immigrants, for the most part feeling Americanized (and relatively unconscious about how their presence may have redefined that term), exhibit a degree of uncertainty about what to make of those who comprise the latest immigrants. Will the benefits of having them here outweigh the costs? Will they assimilate and become more like "us"? Does their presence aid or hurt in economic competition, a process now perceived by most citizens as

v

a dog-eat-dog international struggle? Those in public life inevitably speculate about whether the many potential new citizens and voters will alter the balance of power in politics. And, at all levels of government, there is concern about the impact of immigration on budgets, schools, and crime.

In the past decade, these old questions and many others have been focused on the very large Hispanic, especially Mexican, immigration to the United States. The Hispanic population counted in the 1990 census included 7.8 million people born in other countries. This attention, of course, is not because a substantial Hispanic population is a new phenomenon, particularly in the Southwest. (The census also revealed more than 14 million native-born Hispanic Americans.) It is, in fact, merely the latest expression of adjustment, uneasiness, and uncertainty caused by renewed large scale change in the nation's population.

In the pages that follow, Roberto Suro, the staff writer responsible for covering immigration issues at the *Washington Post*, strikes exactly the right balance on this point, conceiving his mission broadly and going well beyond the particulars of recent Hispanic immigration to set it in the context of the history of American immigration and the evolution of public policy in this area. Suro's survey of current American policy reveals both the similarities with past policy debates and the special factors that are present in a more mature, more economically stressed America of the 1990s. Suro examines and explains the conflicting evidence regarding the economic impact of immigrants and offers specific recommendations for shifts in policy, including a tax on immigrants.

Suro's central message is that the real challenge of immigration is not control of entry but rather what to do about the immigrants who succeed in reaching the United States. In other words, how will any group be integrated into the economic mainstream of American life. Suro argues, in effect, that we need to ask how many people we want to admit, in the context of what are we prepared to do with and for them once they are here. This involves an examination of the social contract as it affects recent immigrants—a discussion of special importance given the changes in attitudes toward the public sector over the past two decades.

Suro's paper on Hispanic immigration is related to several other research programs under way at the Twentieth Century Fund. Recent Twentieth Century Fund papers like Robert Pastor's *Integration with Mexico: Options for U.S. Policy* and Peter Morici's *Free Trade in the Americas* address growing trade integration in the Western hemisphere—a development closely tied to immigration. In addition, last year we published Thomas Muller's *Immigrants in the American City*, and we recently commissioned a book from Saskia Sassen on immigrants in the global economy.

Suro's effort will not only increase public understanding of the nature of immigration to America, but will also help sharpen the debate over immigration policy. On behalf of the Trustees, I thank him for his work and insight on this important topic.

Richard C. Leone, *President*
The Twentieth Century Fund
June 1994

CONTENTS

FOREWORD BY RICHARD C. LEONE   v

ACKNOWLEDGMENTS   x

I   A NATION OF IMMIGRANTS, AGAIN

CHAPTER 1   THE WORLD IN MOTION   3

CHAPTER 2   AFTER THE PAUSE   9

CHAPTER 3   CREATORS, IMPORTERS, AND POOR RELATIONS   21

II   ENTRY: THE INTERNATIONAL DYNAMIC

CHAPTER 4   FROM WHERE? AND WHY?   31

CHAPTER 5   TRAVELING FOR A FAMILY   35

CHAPTER 6   TRAVELING THE CHANNELS   41

CHAPTER 7   THE MEXICAN CASE   47

CHAPTER 8   TOWARD A POLICY OF ENTRY   53

III   INTEGRATION: A DOMESTIC AFFAIR

CHAPTER 9   BEYOND THE MELTING POT AND THE MOSAIC   63

CHAPTER 10   IMMIGRATION TO THE BURN ZONE   71

CHAPTER 11   ILLEGAL ALIENS, ILLEGAL JOBS   85

CHAPTER 12   DEBATING THE COSTS OF IMMIGRATION   93

CHAPTER 13   TOWARD A POLICY OF INTEGRATION   101

NOTES   115

INDEX   119

ABOUT THE AUTHOR   125

ACKNOWLEDGMENTS

The reporting and writing of this paper was supported by fellowships from the Alicia Patterson Foundation, the California State University, and the Woodrow Wilson Center; and the Twentieth Century Fund was responsible for the publication as well as providing support for the writing. I am deeply grateful to these institutions and absolve them of any responsibility for the outcome. In addition, I owe special thanks to four friends who read an early draft of the manuscript and greatly improved it with their suggestions: Demetrios Papademetriou, senior associate at the Carnegie Endowment for International Peace; James D. Calaway, a Houston entrepreneur; Barry Munitz, chancellor of the California State University; and Ruben Armiñana, president of Sonoma State University. I must also thank my editors at the *Washington Post* for their unfailing graciousness. And finally I am most indebted to my wife, Mary, for her loving sustenance.

I

A Nation of Immigrants, Again

CHAPTER 1

THE WORLD IN MOTION

At the immigration museum on Ellis Island, just beyond the huge hall where shiploads of newcomers once claimed their baggage, there now stands a giant globe with a lot of little white lights on it. The lights go on and off in sequence to illustrate patterns of migration at different points in modern history.

The lights come in waves, building, cresting, halting, giving way to other movements. People are scattered to new lands by empire-building in the eighteenth century and then by industrialization in the nineteenth and the beginning of the twentieth centuries. At moments the globe is dim, signifying times when few people moved.

This ebb and flow of the lights illustrate two things clearly: The history of migration is not a continuous flux but a series of episodes, each with a beginning, middle, and end. And when migration does take place it usually involves people leaving many places for many different destinations rather than just a singular, linear movement from one nation to another.

If the Ellis Island exhibit were fully updated to reflect migration patterns at the end of the twentieth century, the globe would look like an apparition from the Las Vegas strip. It would have so many little trails of lights flashing from one spot to another that the world would seem ablaze with motion.

In Africa, the lights would stream across the fat part of the continent from east to west, from the center toward the south, and from the north across the Mediterranean to Europe. The former Soviet Union would be a swirl of white dots. From Eastern Europe, especially from the former Yugoslavia, streams of lights would converge in Germany. Long arcs of lights would stretch across the seas to the Arabian Peninsula from the Indian subcontinent, Korea, the Philippines, and the Levant. Odd strands of lights would crisscross Asia, to represent perhaps the large flow of people from Indonesia to Malaysia and the lesser migration from Malaysia to Japan. South Korea would be both a destination and a departure point. From Vietnam and the Philippines, the flows would blossom out in many directions.

The most concentrated course of lights would be from a few places in Latin America to a few destinations in the United States. The brightest single connection anywhere on the globe, a radiant display of human movement, would be between Mexico and southern California.

According to a 1992 World Bank estimate, some one hundred million people are living outside of their native lands for one reason or another, as immigrants in some foreign nation.[1] Many millions more have left their homes to live elsewhere in their own countries, most shifting from rural areas to the new megacities of the Third World. This vast displacement of people constitutes the most complex and extensive period of migration in human history.[2] The movement of peoples is a defining characteristic of our age.

THE VISIBLE FACE OF CHANGE

In 1993 a report by the United Nations Population Fund proclaimed that "migration is the visible face of social change,"[3] a statement that can be taken in its broadest sense. Migration is a symptom of change, but it is also both a cause and an effect of change. Migration helped bring down the Berlin Wall, and it has been a major consequence of its fall. An abundant supply of foreign workers spurred the growth of the U.S. low-wage service industries, and the availability of those jobs acted as a magnet for further immigration.

Aside from the political and economic changes, migration is prompted by other kinds of change that are more difficult to measure. Distance, for example, is no longer a matter of miles. Time is no longer measured in hours. Consider the case of Katrina, a young woman who grew up in a village near Bogota, Colombia, where most people work growing flowers for export to the United States. Early one morning in April 1992, she set out for the United States from her family home armed with a tourist visa, which she had no intention of honoring. By early evening she was looking for a job as a baby-sitter in northern New Jersey. As she traveled, she hummed the latest Madonna tune and daydreamed about how she would spend her first paycheck at a suburban mall, buying things she had seen a thousand times on television. How far is it from the Province of Cundinamarca to Bergen County? And how long does it really take to get there? Katrina was already very close before she left.

Other change can come about for less obvious reasons. The populations of the industrialized societies of the Northern Hemisphere have almost stopped growing, while in the South human life is becoming ever more plentiful.

Ostensibly a reflection of economic circumstances, these drastic differences in fertility rates must also reflect contrasting attitudes toward a primordial human function. Meanwhile, all over the world, in rapidly growing nations just as much as in those with stable or even declining populations, women have drastically redefined their place in the family and in society, reflecting global changes in the most basic human relationships. Migration accompanies all these changes.

It is an enduring truth of human behavior that when confronted with change some people move. They move not to escape change but to adapt to it. A growing body of evidence from current and past migration shows that often an individual's decision to move is just one part of a much broader economic strategy carried out by friends and relatives who never leave home. The extent to which the migration drama plays itself out in the old country, not in the new one, is signaled by the massive sums of money that immigrants send home. A recent UN study calculated that remittances by immigrants worldwide constitute an international flow of money second only to the sums associated with the purchase of crude oil.[4]

A NEW WAVE OF MIGRATION

The United States prides itself on being a "nation of immigrants," and, perhaps more than any other modern nation, it has been shaped by the movement of peoples. But immigration has not been a constant in U.S. history. It has taken place in clearly identifiable waves, each with distinct characteristics and each with a different impact on the nation.

This volume begins with the assumptions that a new era of immigration to the United States is now fully under way, that this immigration is already too large an event to ignore, and that it is an event as yet too new to easily understand.

As a purely contemporary phenomenon, today's migration is no more than a distant cousin to the mythic era of immigration from Europe. Like its predecessors, however, the current wave is drastically reshaping the United States. It is innately associated with the political, economic, cultural, and demographic changes now so quickly reshaping the world. No description can be definitive, no prediction final.

The current wave of migration is not an undifferentiated mass movement of people from poor countries to rich ones. No era of migration is quite so simple. Instead, the movement of peoples takes place along channels formed by a variety of relationships between the sending and receiving nations, involving culture, trade, diplomatic ties, and other factors. Migrations need to be understood and managed in terms of these linkages, and today they are more complex than any that came before.

When the big globe at Ellis Island illustrates the European migration to the United States around the turn of the century, a thick band of white lights makes a stately march across the Atlantic. It is an accurate portrayal because during that time manufactured goods, capital, technology, culture, ideologies, and people all pretty much traveled in the same direction, from east to west, from Europe to America. All at a steamship's pace.

To reflect the situation today, the globe would have to a show an intricate web of instant communications. Goods and capital dart back and forth among nations. Political influence and military might streak across distances long and short. Culture radiates in increasingly powerful beams from an ever-smaller number of sources, most of them in the United States. All these global traffic patterns manifest themselves at least in part in migration.

Much of the current migration to the United States reflects a two-way traffic. The United States has sent out armies (as in the case of Vietnam), engaged in trade (as in the case of China), or both (as happened with Korea). In return it has received people. This two-way traffic can develop very quickly, as happened with the Dominican Republic after the 1965 U.S. military intervention. Also, the numbers of people traveling along old, well-established routes can explode quite suddenly, as happened with Mexico in the 1980s.

With so many factors prompting and directing human flows, perhaps the most remarkable characteristic of current migration to the United States is that so much of it comes from a single region of the world. The nations of Latin America are the source of almost all the large, well-established, contemporary movements of people to this country. Asia has produced three migrations that share those same characteristics, the flows from China, India, and the Philippines, but altogether these three vast and populous nations account for fewer immigrants than the comparatively tiny islands of the Caribbean, when estimates for illegal immigration are added in.

This study focuses primarily on Hispanic immigration, not only because of the numbers involved but also because of the important and distinct policy challenges it presents. Sheer proximity makes it difficult to regulate a flow of people from Latin America because of the large numbers of illegal border crossers as well as people who claim political asylum upon reaching U.S. territory.

While Asian immigration embraces a rainbow of ethnic and linguistic identities, Latino migrants have enough in common that they often stand out in the prism of U.S. politics as a single group with unique characteristics. For this reason, Latino immigrants are certain to have a strong influence on the course of American life for the next fifty years.

The Latino population counted in the 1990 census included 7.8 million people born in other countries, in addition to more than 14 million native-born Americans. The Latino population therefore is composed of newcomers

struggling to find their way in the United States as well as members of an ethnic minority that has a long history of unhappy dealings with the Anglo mainstream. Together these groups of Latino Americans are numerous enough to
demand attention, and they are growing so fast that they will soon exercise
real power.

Yet this Hispanic American community faces exceptional difficulties in
establishing its place in the U.S. civic society. More than any minority group,
it must contend with the challenges of integrating a large number of immigrants, including many illegal aliens. And more than any other immigrant
group, Latinos must contend with the challenges of minority group status.
These difficulties are especially acute because this wave of Latino immigration coincides with a period of confusion and controversy among native-born
Americans as to the place of immigration in the nation's civic life.

These challenges are compounded by the fact that Latino immigration
includes a sizable portion of people condemned always to work hard for low
wages and whose lives hover dangerously close to the oblivion of the urban
underclass. Many are locked into this existence because they entered the country illegally, others because they lack education and skills. This rapid growth of
the low-wage work force is one of the most serious threats to the well-being of
the Hispanic community and to the nation as a whole, especially when the
presence of illegal aliens permits abuses by employers. As such, the most important dilemmas posed by unlawful migrations are ultimately economic choices,
rather than law enforcement challenges.

IMMIGRATION AT A TIME OF RESTRUCTURING

The fact that today's immigrants arrive in the midst of a drastic restructuring of the U.S. labor force is one of the major concerns for the nation. A
strong back and a willingness to work no longer qualify an immigrant for
upward mobility. As the economy changes there are ever-fewer jobs that allow
an immigrant entry into the middle class.

The greatest challenges posed by this lack of mobility lie not so much
with the immigrants as with their children. They are growing up as Americans
in big cities beset with crime, drugs, and collapsing school systems and other
social services. They are acculturating to the sickest part of U.S. society and
graduating into a labor force that offers no more than life at the bottom. One
reason so many children are in this condition is that recent Latino immigrants
are the most fertile segment of the population.

Immigration suffuses the American identity, and informs all the nation's
history and culture. Immigrants, from the Puritans to Einstein, are a mythic
archetype in the American pantheon. They have validated the nation at every
turn its history merely by choosing to come here.

Like most myths, however, this is based on a distant past, and to glance backward now can be disorienting. The United States is not necessarily better suited to dealing with immigration today because it was a nation of immigrants before. History helps in understanding some of the enduring human behaviors and some of the broad patterns common to every age of immigration. But immigration is not fundamentally an American historical phenomenon. Today it is a global event deeply intertwined with contemporary political, economic, and social forces.

As always, immigration holds out great promise and great peril. Change is the only certainty in such a massive demographic event. Immigration is here, immigration is happening, but the outcome is far from certain. Immigration cannot be avoided. The challenge is to make it work.

CHAPTER 2

AFTER THE PAUSE

I t was a time of high anxiety over immigration. The federal government had tried several ways to stem the tide, but the flood of newcomers seemed unstoppable. Not only were the numbers growing, but the immigrants were different from the native-born Americans. They were dark and ethnic, and across the country Americans blamed them for taking jobs and for disrupting communities with their strange ways, their narrow group interests, and their exotic ideologies.

Finally Congress got tough. The chief sponsor of legislation designed to end the influx of southern and eastern European immigrants that had been building since the turn of the century crowed, "The day of unalloyed welcome to all peoples, the day of indiscriminate acceptance of all races has definitely ended." That was seventy years ago, and the voice belonged to Senator Albert Johnson of Washington.[1] His National Origins Act of 1924 created a system of strict new annual quotas.

The law worked. It almost immediately cut the flow to a fifth of what it had been before World War I, although intended mainly to cut the more recent influx of undesirable nationalities while leaving the door open to "traditional" immigrants such as those from Great Britain, Ireland, and Germany. Then two great events brought the era of European immigration to a definitive close: the Great Depression and World War II. Before and during the war the United States effectively closed its doors to those fleeing fascism, and afterward only a small portion of the displaced masses of Europe and Asia were granted haven.

For more than fifty years after the enactment of the 1924 law, the United States experienced exceptionally low levels of immigration. Between the turn

9

of the century and World War I, when European immigration was at its peak, the United States admitted an average of more than 950,000 immigrants a year. During the long pause in migration from the mid-1920s until the late 1970s, the average was fewer than 250,000 a year.

This extraordinary hiatus is one of the central facts that define the current wave of migration. We are witnessing a new event. No matter how fast human history seems to be racing at the end of the twentieth century, almost all developments are in fact evolutionary, whether in science or technology or culture. In all these areas progress can be measured step by step, and for the most part people have time to adjust. The current wave of immigration, however, does not build on the past. It did not evolve out of the European immigration that ended in 1924. Rather, it is both sui generis and sudden. And it is a huge event, accounting for more than a third of the nation's population growth going into the 1990s.

The current wave of immigration was made possible in 1965, when Congress fundamentally rewrote the nation's immigration laws dispatching the racially motivated quota laws that had been in place since 1924. The influx gradually built strength during the 1970s and then developed enormous momentum in the 1980s. More immigrants, a million and a half more, entered the country legally between 1975 and 1992 than during the preceding fifty years (see Figure 2.1).

FIGURE 2.1
IMMIGRATION BY DECADE
1820–1980

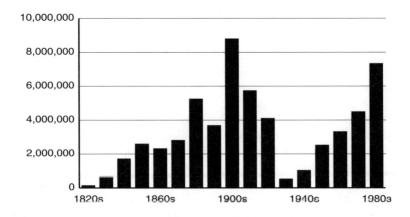

Source: U.S. Department of Justice, *Statistical Yearbook of the Immigration and Naturalization Service*, 1992.

If massive immigration seems novel to many people today, perhaps even frightening, there is a simple explanation: It is indeed a new experience for this country. The years between the 1920s and the 1990s are an eternity in U.S. history. During this long hiatus immigration became enshrined in myth, yet the United States forgot how to be a nation of immigrants.

Like Rip van Winkle aroused from his slumbers, the United States is trying to understand an event that is at once familiar but different from any before. The nation's reference points for the massive immigration it is once again in the business of managing are set in an era of steamships and telegraphs, but now it is taking place in a time of jet travel and global television. The world is different, the country is different, and the very nature of immigration is different. Instead of adding Europeans to a population primarily of European extraction, current immigration brings in nationalities and ethnic groups that previously represented only small parts of the nation's population.

ENTRY AND INTEGRATION

Sudden and massive, the influx of people now under way obliges the United States to invent itself once more as a nation of immigrants. This volume addresses the beginning of that process rather than its end, and instead of trying to prescribe immigration policy for the future, attempts to define the challenges. It offers some criteria designed to make immigration a more manageable subject and suggests some broad principles around which a serious and productive policy discussion can take place.

To start, it is important to divide the process of migration into two distinct phases—entry and integration. Each is a process with its own dynamics, and each requires its own responses from government and society. At this point, well into a period of massive immigration, the United States does not have public policies or private institutions that function effectively in either realm.

The first phase of migration, *entry*, is the process of arriving in the United States. Why do people come? Why do they come from some countries and not from others? The answers to these questions should help determine how the nation manages the flow of people and how it goes about the process of accepting some, turning away some, and discouraging others from even trying to come. Understanding the process of entry tells us a lot about what is happening and what lies ahead, and it can provide a critical set of facts to direct implementation of immigration policies. But merely understanding the process of entry is not the same as setting immigration policies, explaining their purposes, or defining their ultimate results.

The second part, *integration*, is the process by which the immigrant finds a place in the United States. What happens to migrants once they are here? What spaces are available to them in our economy and our civic life? What becomes of their children? The answers to these questions would help both government and society to determine what they are willing to do to ensure that these newcomers make a positive contribution to American life. Understanding the process of integration tells us a lot about the costs and benefits of massive immigration. Determining the requirements for successful integration should be the essential first step toward deciding how many migrants the nation can absorb. Integration happens on U.S. soil, and successful integration requires a positive effort by the people already living in the United States. Any nation runs obvious risks if it lets huge numbers of people through its borders and airports with no regard as to how to integrate them effectively and humanely. Yet that is the risk the United States is running today.

FOR WANT OF A POLICY

Ideally, the United States should have a clear sense of purpose and well-articulated goals when it undertakes a challenge such as managing a massive immigration. At the very least, the public should have a general feeling that such an immigration suits the national interest.

Unfortunately, nearly a century has passed since the United States had either a clear goal or definable purposes for its immigration policies. Up to the 1890s the purpose was to populate the nation, and the goal was to absorb as many able-bodied people as possible. Since then, Washington has developed a large and arcane canon of numerologies that masquerades as a policy. There are national quotas, preference categories, and an alphabet soup of visa and adjustment categories, from A11's to XN3's. There is, however, no coherence. Every effort at precision has been interlaced with exceptions, exemptions, or special categories, because at every turn politics has intervened in favor of ambiguity.

Even though the politics of immigration have changed many times since the 1890s, the United States has never articulated an immigration policy with an overall purpose, nor has it ever stated unequivocally, "This many and no more." The government's only unmistakable statements have been in regard to specific groups. At different times it has tried to exclude all sorts of nationalities, such as the Chinese, the Italians, and the Turks. It has also tried to block certain individuals deemed subversive, from John Lennon to diehard Leninists. Meanwhile, the government has also made a variety of special provisions, for groups such as Mexican farm workers, refugees from Communist countries, children fathered by U.S. servicemen in Vietnam, and former employees of the Panama Canal Company.

Immigration is not unlike federal tax policy. The overall goal can only be stated so broadly that it is meaningless: "Everyone should pay their fair share to support government." Or "Immigration is part of our national heritage."

Then what? At the level of federal policy, nothing. No other honest statement is possible because any sense of purpose and strategy has been lost in a thicket of detailed provisions and exceptions. As with Washington's budget deficit, many elected officials make a lot of strong statements about immigration, especially during times of economic crisis, but few ever offer an overall strategy for dealing with it. This is especially true when such a strategy might involve political or economic costs. This is painfully apparent in examining the recent history of the three major fields of immigration policy: combating illegal immigration, administering programs for refugees or asylum seekers, and regulating legal immigration.

ILLEGAL IMMIGRATION

For most of its history the United States has not had a policy on illegal immigration because it was not considered a problem. Until the 1920s, the Border Patrol did not exist and people coming across the land borders were not even counted. Since then, and especially during good times, Mexicans in particular have often been encouraged to come across as migrant workers. Some 4.5 million Mexicans worked in the fields of California and the Southwest under the *bracero*, or temporary worker, program begun in 1942 to deal with wartime labor shortages and extended until 1964 as a source of cheap field hands. During economic hard times in the 1930s and 1950s, the federal government simply rounded up Mexican workers and sent them home, at gunpoint if necessary.

By 1980 both the open door and mass deportations had become politically untenable, so Congress began what would become a six-year debate over the nation's first explicit policy toward illegal immigration. The result was the Immigration Reform and Control Act (IRCA) of 1986, a law as ambivalent in its intent and as ambiguous in its results as any ever enacted.

In order to control a rapidly growing influx of undocumented migrants, the law for the first time imposed sanctions on the employers who gave them jobs. In order to avoid mass deportations and to allow people to come out of the shadows, the law also declared an amnesty for people who had lived here illegally since at least 1982. And to satisfy California fruit growers, who complained that they would be denied the cheap work force on which they depended, the law broadened the amnesty to cover people who could claim they had worked in the fields.

The amnesty was implemented with considerable success, providing legal status to nearly three million people, about 60 percent of the total illegal population at the time. However, since the 1986 reform no president and no Congress has been willing to commit significant funds to the enforcement of employer sanctions. The ban on the employment of illegal aliens is a prohibition with no teeth, and it is widely flouted. By most estimates, the size of the illegal population has been growing steadily since the amnesty was implemented and now approaches four million people.[2]

The government's ability to actually control illegal immigration can be discussed only hypothetically because Washington has never made full use of the tools already in the statute books. The Clinton administration's 1992 initiative on illegal immigration focused primarily on increased funding for the Border Patrol with only token sums going to the enforcement of employer sanctions. This strategy assumes that illegal immigration is a problem of entry and that the challenge is to "keep them out." In fact, the crisis is one of integration. The front lines in this battle are not along the Rio Grande but in the urban sweatshops where employers are all to happy to employ illegal aliens at poverty wages. In the absence of any commitment to enforce the 1986 law, all proclamations about the sanctity of borders verge on hypocrisy.

So the flow of people illegally entering the nation continues. Though only marginally affected by government policy, the persistent and growing population of undocumented migrants skews the entire discussion of immigration policy. The very presence of this population sows confusion, allowing people to put legal and illegal immigrants into one pot of suspect and undeserving foreigners. It introduces the rhetoric and emotions of law enforcement to the immigration debate.

REFUGEES AND ASYLUM SEEKERS

Until the 1960s the United States never faced the challenge of serving as a nation of first asylum. Previously it almost always dealt with refugees who had already escaped their homeland and who sought admission to the United States from a third country that had already given them shelter. All this changed after Cubans, and then Haitians and Central Americans, turned up on the country's shores or at its borders seeking haven from political persecution.

In the 1980s and early 1990s, the United States often responded to this challenge inconsistently. For a while, Washington welcomed Nicaraguans fleeing the Sandinistas but shunned Salvadorans fleeing right-wing death squads. Then it tried to restrain the Nicaraguans and later created a generous program for Salvadorans. The asylum system was repeatedly revised and expanded, but it constantly fell behind, creating a backlog of undecided cases expected to reach a million people in 1994. As a result, civil rights and immigration advocates successfully brought a number of class-action lawsuits against the federal government, charging that it failed to deal either fairly or effectively with asylum seekers.

In early 1994 the Clinton administration crafted the fourth major proposal since 1986 for expanding and streamlining the asylum system. This plan was the result of the trial and error of the past and a greater consultation with interest groups than any before. But it still devoted only modest resources to a large and growing challenge.

The moral fractures in that policy are evident almost every day in the Straits of Florida. All Cubans who make it to the United States are assumed to be fleeing political persecution, and so they are put in a special category that allows them to be "adjusted" into full, permanent legal status. This continues despite the fact that many of those arriving from Cuba today readily admit they've been happy to live with Fidel Castro for more than thirty years and that they left only because the economic conditions have of late become intolerable. Nonetheless, they are automatically welcomed as escapees from an enemy ideology.

Haiti, meanwhile, has a more violently repressive regime than Cuba, but anyone arriving from this country is assumed to be immigrating for economic benefit. Unless Haitians can provide specific evidence that they have reason to fear persecution, they are assumed to be unworthy of admission.

In 1980 Congress adopted the Geneva Convention definition of a refugee as a person with a "well-founded fear of persecution," and that remains the standard for admission both for refugees screened abroad and for asylum seekers who apply once they are in the United States. As noble as that standard may seem, it has often been interpreted to fit foreign policy goals and domestic political constraints in ways that rob refugee and asylum policy of any coherence.

For example, nearly five years after the collapse of Communism, almost half of those admitted as refugees continue to arrive from the former Soviet Union and Vietnam. Regardless of whether they individually merit protection (and many undoubtedly do), this preference remains in place primarily as a legacy of the Cold War. Meanwhile, other cases, such as China, Haiti, and El Salvador, have been treated almost exclusively on an ad hoc basis. Sometimes the door is left open a bit. Sometimes it is shut tight.

The lack of a clearly articulated policy has made it difficult to arouse political support for refugee and asylum programs. To make matters worse, in 1993 the World Trade Center bombing and the smuggling ships from China drove home an impression that the asylum system is subject to wholesale abuse. Meanwhile, thousands of asylum seekers wait in limbo to learn the fate of their applications, which flounder in the ever-growing backlog of cases.

The Clinton reform proposals attempt to remedy the worst problems of the asylum system and to begin the long process of working through a backlog. Even if the reform works as advertised, it will take years to repair the damage done to the public's perception of the asylum system.

More than any other form of immigration policy, the decision whether to grant safe haven expresses a moral judgment about the individual. Like St. Peter at the pearly gates, the government decides who is worthy of entering and receiving protection and who is cast out. Yet the United States has no clearly stated political criteria for these judgments, and in many other cases the government simply finds itself unable to render a judgment at all.

LEGAL IMMIGRATION

Even in the largest field of immigration policy, the admission of legal immigrants, the government takes a position of singular ambiguity.

Congress first opened the doors to legal immigration from Latin America and Asia in 1965, when it repealed the quota system adopted in 1924 that favored northern Europeans. The new law developed as a civil rights initiative to purge the ethnic and racial bias of the National Origins Act. Washington eliminated policies that had repugnant racial overtones, but it had no new policies to cope with massive immigration. Indeed, there was little immigration then, there had not been for forty years, and there was no reason to assume it would suddenly increase.

Against this backdrop of civil rights reform and low immigration, the United States developed a policy framework that greatly favors the relatives of citizens in granting immigrant visas. Leaving aside the one-time amnesty for illegals in the 1986 law, nearly two-thirds of all remaining ongoing immigration falls under into the family category (see Figure 2.2).

As immigration reached numbers not seen since the early years of this century, Congress attempted to enact a new policy framework for legal immigration with the Immigration Act of 1990. The original intent was to set limits on overall immigration and to increase the number of visas set aside for

FIGURE 2.2
CATEGORIES OF IMMIGRATION
Fiscal Year 1992

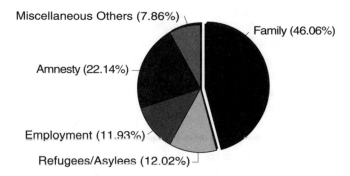

Source: U.S. Department of Justice, *Statistical Yearbook of the Immigration and Naturalization Service,* 1992.

investors and workers with needed skills. Instead, the bill became a "Christmas tree," in Capitol Hill parlance, as legislators hung it with a variety of exceptions promoted by interest groups ranging from Mexican Americans to the Irish community of Boston to international banks with large numbers of employees in Hong Kong. Rather than creating a cohesive policy, the law added many new categories of favored immigrants. In intense deal making, the legislators created a "pierceable cap," which sets a nominal ceiling on immigration (initially 675,000 persons a year) and then creates mechanisms to breach this number, primarily through some categories of unlimited family immigration.

Family dynamics ultimately determine how many immigrants enter legally each year and where they come from. Decisions are not made by any government strategists or by the invisible hand of the marketplace. Since immigrants can become citizens, and as citizens they gain the right to bring in their relatives, this policy creates a self-perpetuating chain of immigration based on kinship. This ensures that immigrant flows from specific countries, even from specific communities, will grow exponentially. For more than 400,000 new entrants a year, the demographic core of the current phase of migration, it is the immigrants themselves who regulate immigration policy.

Even though family reunification is terribly important to those suffering separation from their loved ones, it is a concern not shared by the vast majority of Americans, who will never be in the position of sponsoring an immigrant. As a result, family-based immigration is a policy with no broad constituency. Defenders of the system argue that an immigrant arriving with family sponsorship is backed by a ready-made support system more effective than any bureaucracy designed to help newcomers find work and housing. But both the logic of family immigration and its relatively small constituency mean that it has no readily recognized claim on government resources. Family-based immigration may prove to serve the nation well, but it does not now project an obvious sense of purpose.

This lack of policy direction would be no great loss except for the fact that the United States faces an era of prolonged, sustained, large-scale immigration with profound societal implications. The current wave of migration, particularly Latino immigration, is already changing our society. Even if immigration simply continues at its current pace for another two or three decades, it will be one of the defining forces in U.S. history for the whole of the twenty-first century.

Already, the changes brought by immigration are provoking fear and anxiety in some quarters. Such feelings intensify and are more easily manipulated for political ends when the federal government seems incapable of controlling the influx. Given the ineluctable link between demographic change and fear, the absence of any coherent policy guarantees only that immigration will become a larger, more contentious issue in the future. The question is, What would justify an effort to develop a national consensus around a comprehensive set of policies?

During the late 1980s the United States absorbed a steady flow of about a million immigrants a year, including the undocumented. Even if the flow declines, the nation stands to take in eight or nine million newcomers in the 1990s. That is roughly equivalent to the population of Ohio, and that alone, without the need to proclaim a crisis, should justify a reexamination of our national goals and methods in managing immigration.

One indication of how unprepared the nation is to deal with this immense wave of immigration is the continued use of an obsolete vocabulary to describe it. Most of the concepts applied to the integration of immigrants harken back to the era of European immigration and before, for instance, to the ever popular idea that the United States is a melting pot. Some other strategies are drawn from the United States' tortured efforts to harmonize racial differences, such as the appeals to multiculturalism as a way for dealing with immigrants' diverse cultures. There are lessons to be drawn from history in both cases, but one cannot expect to find functioning models for contemporary immigration by reaching back thirty years to Mississippi or eighty years to lower Manhattan.

With immigration intruding into debates over everything from welfare reform to earthquake relief, it had become evident by early 1994 that the federal government needed once again to reassess its immigration policies. It is increasingly likely that the Congress that will be elected in November 1994 will seriously address immigration even though it may take years to enact major legislation.

What the nation can hope for out of this process is that immigration policy will be rebuilt from the ground up. This would require developing a set of goals, purposes, and strategies both to regulate the entry of immigrants and to ensure their successful integration. The nation might then face the challenges ahead calmly and with confidence.

Two major goals related to both the entry and integration of the immigrant should guide this process of reevaluation:

First, given the potential for increasing migration pressures around the world, the United States cannot wait passively to see who shows up at its door. The most far-reaching way to control immigration is through foreign policy. Reducing migration pressures should be a major goal across the gamut of foreign policy, from trade and development to human rights and military aid. Particular priority should be given to minimizing the risk of catastrophic migrations—sudden, massive, and uncontrolled influxes—which put the most strain on the nation's ability to integrate migrants and cause the greatest political disruption.

However, citizens and leaders alike must realize that a nation can try to manage immigrant flows, but that no government can absolutely control immigration. It can try to gradually shift the momentum, but it cannot turn it on and off like a water spigot. It can nip and squeeze and push and pressure in order to guide an influx, but no government can state categorically that a specific number of immigrants will come from certain countries. Yet even accepting these limitations, no government can afford to ignore immigration.

Second, immigration should be perceived as a vast social enterprise that affects the entire country, so there is a clear national interest in making it a successful venture. But the costs of successful immigration need to be assessed carefully because many will be paid up front before any benefits are realized.

Consequently, the nation must engage in a series of calculations and decide among three broad options.

The first is to gauge the number of people who should be granted entry according to a very explicit estimate of what the nation wants to spend to ensure their successful integration.

The second option is to follow the present course and allow a large number of immigrants to fall into the urban underclass. This means having to pay the costs of maintaining them and their progeny in a life of poverty and alienation.

The third option is to pay the very substantial costs, both monetary and social, of attempting vastly to curtail immigration into the United States.

Each of these options is expensive, but as we will see, the most expensive option may well be to continue along the aimless course the United States has pursued since the current wave of immigration began.

The world is on the move, and the United States is one of the main destinations. To sleep while a substantial wave of immigrants enters the country is simply to invite a rude awakening later.

CHAPTER 3

CREATORS, IMPORTERS, AND POOR RELATIONS

The history of the United States as a nation of immigrants is commonly divided into what the historian John Higham described as "two large and quite distinct phases."[1] The first lasted roughly from the 1680s to 1803, and the second from the 1820s until European immigration dwindled in the 1920s.

By these standards the United States is now clearly experiencing a third phase of immigration, whose impact will be at least as great as the first two. The current phase can be dated to the mid-1960s, when Congress opened the doors to massive family-based legal immigration from Latin America and Asia. It was also when Mexican farm workers, long accustomed to entering the country under the temporary worker, or *bracero*, program, started coming illegally in ever greater numbers. The mid-1960s also marked the peak of the postwar manufacturing economy and the start of a restructuring process still under way. And it marked a time when the last immigrants of the European wave began leaving the work force. In response to these and many other factors the numbers of immigrants began to grow quickly, with the pace accelerating into the early 1990s (see Figure 3.1, page 22).

Each of the three waves of immigration has come during very different eras in the nation's history, and each has brought in very different kinds of migrants. Consequently, each migration presented its own distinct challenges. One way to define the character of the current migration and to assess its potential impact is to compare it to the prior eras. Each wave has demanded that the nation find new ways of admitting and absorbing foreigners, and in each case the response has been different.

The first wave of immigration took place during the colonial period and initial settlement of the country. The second coincided with the nation's urban development and its industrialization. The third is occurring during the suburban boom and the emergence of a postindustrial economy.

As for the immigrants themselves, Higham notes some broad differences between the first two phases: "Whereas the First Immigration had been entirely white and predominantly English-speaking, the Second brought a Babel of tongues and an array of complexions ranging from the bland Scandinavian through the swarthy south Italian to the West Indian Negro. And whereas the First Immigration had been very largely Protestant, the Second was heavily Catholic from the outset and by the end of the century it was increasingly Jewish and Eastern Orthodox."[2]

FIGURE 3.1
LEGAL IMMIGRATION
Yearly Totals 1960–1992

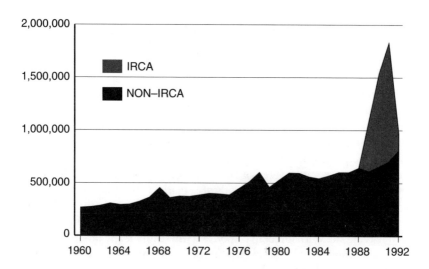

Source: U.S. Department of Justice, Statistical Yearbook of the Immigration and Naturalization Service, 1992.

AND NOW THE LATINOS

The content of the third and current phase is equally distinctive because so much of the influx is composed of a single linguistic and regional group—Latin Americans (see Figure 3.2).

During the 1980s some 47 percent of all legal immigration came from Latin America. When estimates of the illegal migration are added to the numbers of legal entries, the Hispanic share goes much higher, up to 60 percent to 70 percent of the total influx.

The other major component of the current wave came from Asia and accounts for about 37 percent of legal immigration. But the Asian migration is highly fragmented, coming from nations as diverse as India, Korea, the Philippines, and Vietnam. Although Latinos are hardly monolithic, Asian immigrants represent a much starker diversity in terms of economic and political experience, language, culture, and ethnicity.

Not only do Latinos comprise the bulk of the migration, a single nation, Mexico, has accounted for about 28 percent of all legal immigration since 1981 and at least half of the illegal immigration in that time.

FIGURE 3.2
SOURCES OF IMMIGRATION IN THE 1980S

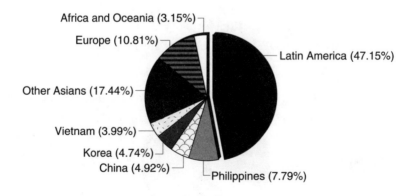

Source: U.S. Department of Justice, *Statistical Yearbook of the Immigration and Naturalization Service, 1992.*

The largest single Asian influx in the 1980s—nearly 550,000 legal immigrants from the Philippines—was barely a third of the 1.6 million legal immigrants from Mexico alone.

No single cultural or linguistic group has so dominated the human traffic to the United States since the British provided some 60 percent of the settlers in the first phase of immigration. During the era of European immigration, there was much more of a mix. In the 1890s, for example, Italy, Russia, Austria-Hungary, and Germany had almost equal shares of the influx, with Scandinavia, Ireland, and Great Britain not far behind (see Figure 3.3).

There are also important differences in the ways that newcomers have related to their new homeland. Higham draws a fine but important distinction between those of one wave, who created colonial America, and those of the next wave, who arrived as foreigners. Regardless of their nationalities, those who arrived prior to the American Revolution "conceived of themselves as founders, settlers, or planters—the formative population of those colonial societies—not as immigrants. Theirs was the polity, the language, the pattern of work and settlement, and many of the mental habits to which the immigrants would have to adjust."

Higham notes the very term *immigrant* did not enter the American lexicon until after the Revolutionary War, when the first immigration was already nearing its end. New arrivals had been called "emigrants," Higham wrote, "but by 1789 our language was beginning to identify newcomers with the country they entered rather than the one they had left. Thus the term *immigrant*

FIGURE 3.3
SOURCES OF IMMIGRATION IN THE 1890S

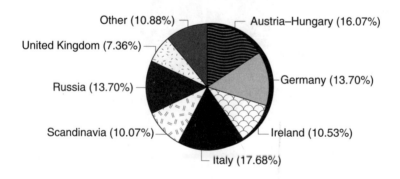

Source: U.S. Department of Justice, *Statistical Yearbook of the Immigration and Naturalization Service,* 1992.

presupposed the existence of a receiving society to which the alien could attach himself. The immigrant is not, then, a colonist or settler who creates a new society and lays down the terms of admission for others. He is rather the bearer of a foreign culture."[3]

In the first phase we had the creators of the baseline American culture, and in the second came those who brought with them—indeed, imported—their own, distinct, foreign cultures.

LATINOS ARRIVING TO A FAMILIAR PLACE

What, then, of the present wave of immigration that is taking place even as American culture and identity are being broadcast into almost every nook and cranny in the world?

Many, arguably most, of this wave of immigrants are thoroughly knowledgeable about contemporary American popular culture even before they arrive. Many, especially among the Latin migrants, have visited here once or more before they have immigrated. Even if it is their first trip here, today's migrants are not going to some place entirely new and different, nor do they arrive as strangers. Instead, they are arriving somewhere that is familiar and that has already helped mold the tastes and aspirations they bring with them. At a minimum they have been watching this culture on television all their lives.

There is yet another level of familiarity as well. Just as the United States has broadcast itself south, Latin America has projected itself to the north.

For many Mexicans, immigration is an act of returning to a place that was once theirs. This in no way reflects irredentist ambitions or Mexican nationalism. It is a cultural and sociological fact, not a political one. Mexicans traveling north see their language and their history all over the landscape. It is no accident that, after more than a century of continuous migration, more than three-quarters of the American population of Mexican descent reside in the broad arc that encompasses San Francisco, Los Angeles, San Diego, Nogales, Santa Fe, Pueblo, El Paso, San Antonio, Corpus Christi, and the city named after the man who first defeated the Mexicans, Houston. Moreover, Latinos coming to these places find their language alive on the radio and in the streets. Their cuisine is in the restaurants. People who look like them and who have the same names are everywhere, in virtually every strata of society.

Even in New York City, Hispanic immigrants find something familiar that is deeply imbedded in the fabric of the city. Moreover, that Latin character is not foreign, especially to the immigrants from the Caribbean. Much of it was put there by Puerto Ricans, native-born Americans who are Latinos.

Latin American immigrants arriving in Miami today find a fully Latinized city that is largely the product of immigration. Modern Miami is a city no older than the Cuban migration that began in the late 1950s, which has done as much to transform its ethnicity as its skyline. The Miami that the migrants encounter today is Latino from its roots.

During the first two waves of migration new arrivals were greeted by robust immigrant societies. In many cases they found old-world-style churches, schools, newspapers, and political organizations operating in their native languages, institutions that were often more pervasive and powerful than their Spanish-speaking counterparts today. However, if one accepts Higham's distinctions, most of those European-style institutions in the first wave actually participated in the creation of a new land, while in the second they were perceived as temporary manifestations of a foreign culture.

The Hispanic culture encountered here by migrants of the third wave has a different quality. It is at once both native and foreign. It is imbedded in the landscape and belongs here, yet remains alien.

The extent to which American culture permeates life in the Latin American countries from which most immigrants come and the permanence of a Latino presence in the United States are two of the factors that make this migration fundamentally different from the ones that came before.

If the migrants of the first wave were the creators and the second were importers, then the Latinos of the third wave come as kinfolk closely related to their new home by geography and history, and by the experiences of native-born Latinos. The Latino migrant today does not traverse an ocean to encounter a new land, but instead crosses a dotted line in the desert to join something familiar. The migrant's voyage in time and space, both literally and in terms of cultural distance, is far shorter for the Latino of the third wave than it was for many of the Europeans or for Asians today.

However, this very familiarity colors the way these new immigrants are perceived. Indeed, if Latinos come as relations, they come as poor relations at best.

IMMIGRATION IN THE POST-CIVIL RIGHTS ERA

During the first two phases of immigration to the United States, the relationship between the newcomers and the new land underwent profound transformations. The colonial era saw efforts to restrict settlement by those considered undesirable or dissimilar, such as the Irish and the Germans. Local conflicts occasionally erupted when the newcomers seemed to be forming distinctive communities. But, as the Revolution approached, the ideologues of independence depicted Americans as a "new breed" that had emerged from a mixture of nationalities. "Europe, and not England, is the parent country of America," was the way Thomas Paine put it in 1776. Very quickly, the claim that Americans were not merely transplanted Englishmen but people of many origins who had come together to form a distinct nation became an important rationale for the revolt against the Crown. Born at a moment when demography and ideology bolstered each other, the concept of the "new breed" also acquired a political dimension because all members of this group were granted equal status. This quickly became a fixture in American political thinking, even if it was not always honored.[4]

So, too, the era of European immigration was characterized by a movement from the rejection of otherness to eventual acceptance. For the entire century that it was under way, this second wave of immigration sparked sometimes violent outbursts of nativism and periodic efforts by government to restrict entry by undesirables. But the idea of Americans as a new breed amalgamated from many nationalities persisted and developed into the myth of the melting pot. Then during the Great Depression and World War II, the influx was shut off and the melting pot became a crucible. By the 1950s, the United States had embraced the ideals of ethnic assimilation. Enduring ethnicity in the form of "hyphenated" Americans was considered benign, even a source of strength, so long as it applied to European nationalities.

The Latino immigrants of the current wave are swept into the maelstrom of unsettled racial issues that in recent years has shattered any notion that all Americans belong to a single, new breed of humanity marked by equality. The newcomers become players in this melodrama because American society fails to distinguish between freshly arrived immigrants and native-born Latinos who have a long history in this country.

Like the Irish and the Germans who migrated continuously for a century or more, Latino newcomers today arrive to find large, well-established communities of their countrymen and coethnics. But there is a difference.

America's barrios were mostly created by native-born Americans of Latino descent with no personal experience of traditional immigration. Latino Americans who trace their roots back to Puerto Rico and Mexico make up three-quarters of the country's Hispanic population. Some of their ancestors became Americans by virtue of conquest rather than by choice. Others took part in informal, often circular migrations of the sort that have taken place between Puerto Rico and New York City since the 1950s. In the first half of this century, similar migrations carried Mexicans all through Texas, the Southwest, California, and beyond.

Although they have very different histories, Native Americans and African Americans are similar to Latino Americans in the sense that all their populations are not derived from traditional immigration. These three groups share two other characteristics that weigh heavily on their present condition.

The first is an extensive history of discrimination, poverty, and powerlessness. The second is that the host society identifies the ethnicity of these groups by socioeconomic status rather than by nationality, culture, or religion, as was the case with European immigrants. As such, Latinos are considered a "minority group," meaning an indigenous population with outstanding grievances against the mainstream society. This is distinct from being an "ethnic group," an appellation increasingly reserved for people of European descent who have willingly assimilated into American culture.

The third wave of immigration began as the United States was belatedly grappling with the issue of race. Coincidentally, the migration has gained momentum during an almost complete breakdown of any consensus on the nature of ethnicity in U.S. society. All of the tensions and confusions that naturally result from an influx of foreigners are playing out against the background of the nation's long, painful, and not entirely successful effort to deal with the legacies of slavery and segregation. The result is that the worlds of politics, popular culture, and academia are riddled with differences over what ethnicity is and what it should be.

These two entirely separate events—Latino immigration and the drama of race relations—have now been fully intermingled, given the position of native-born Latinos as a minority group. More than any other immigrants, Latinos must grapple with the thorny domestic issues that emerge from minority group status. And more than any other minority, Latinos must contend with massive and ongoing immigration. No national or ethnic group has ever had to undertake such a complex feat.

If the past is any guide, the United States can now expect to undergo a prolonged period of ethnic turmoil prompted by a rejection of newcomers. Yet at the same time, the ongoing wave of Latino migration holds the promise of inspiring new approaches to the unresolved issues arising from the troubled African American experience, and may even provide the country with new and more successful ways of managing ethnic relations and urban poverty.

On the other hand, if it all goes badly and Latinos fail to enter the mainstream, this enormous migration could provide the demographic fuel for an era of political and cultural confrontation. If the new migrants and their children are permanently locked into the low-wage economy, the urban underclass would grow quickly and would face not only economic and political disenfranchisement, but also would be cut off linguistically and culturally.

That is the challenge of migration today.

II

Entry: The International Dynamic

CHAPTER 4

FROM WHERE? AND WHY?

The inscription on the Statue of Liberty describes immigrants as the "tired . . . poor . . . the huddled masses yearning to breathe free, the wretched refuse of your teeming shore . . . the homeless, tempest-tossed."

Those words did not fit when Emma Lazarus wrote them in 1883, and they are even less accurate today. Despite the myths of immigration, the poorest of the poor, the most downtrodden and persecuted did not come to the United States during the last wave because they could not make it here or were not allowed in. Things are not much different today.

The tempest-tossed were, and still are, at the mercy of forces beyond their control. It is the others, the ones battling the storms, who take trips. Immigrants are the ones who try to set their own courses, despite the tempests. Throughout U.S. history immigrants have been people with the means and ability to shape their own destinies.

Nearly sixty million people have legally immigrated to the United States since the government began to keep a tally in 1820. Individually, they have probably embodied every motive, base or noble, that the human spirit has invented to justify moving from one place to another. In the aggregate, however, they represent a continuity in human behavior. Their migrations have come about primarily as a response to economic or political upheaval. These are people who sensed that something was changing around them even if they could not understand it. They weighed the relative merits of going or staying, and they decided to go regardless of the obstacles that lay before them.

Understanding how migration functions as a response to a changing world helps explain why some people in some countries come to the United States

31

and others do not. Moreover, examining this response helps identify the types of events that can prompt migration. If there are no answers to the questions "Who comes?" "Why?" and "When?" then there is no way to formulate policies that manage the influx.

People do not leave their homes simply because they are poor, nor do they go somewhere else just because they sense better opportunities there. If either of those statements were in themselves true, a great many more people would be in motion.

In his history of the European wave of immigration, *The Transplanted*, John Bodnar writes, "If immigration was caused largely by the lure of America, then we would expect that struggling people everywhere would come here in relatively equal numbers with common intentions and, for that matter, backgrounds. But historical reality suggests a different explanation to this process. Rates of emigration were not the same everywhere."[1]

Perceptions of economic opportunity in the United States have certainly played an important role all along. And predictably, immigration has flourished in boom times and then shriveled during the Great Depression, as well as various recessions, crises, and crashes. But as Bodnar argues, this does not help explain why immigrants come from some countries and not others. For example, in the 1870s the rate of emigration was twice as heavy from Norway as it was from Sweden.

More tellingly, Bodnar studied regional patterns within individual nations. Throughout the long history of Irish migration to the United States, for instance, the flow of people came from different places at different times but never equally from the entire island all at once. Whether the impetus was the potato famine or competition from imported manufactured goods, levels of emigration varied greatly even in this fairly small country. The one constant over the course of more than two hundred years was that virtually every change produced emigration from somewhere in Ireland. Writing about the European wave, Bodnar concluded, "Movement from areas of either negligible or extremely high poverty was always least."[2]

SENDING AND RECEIVING COMMUNITIES

So too today, Mexico and Colombia send a proportionately greater number of migrants than Honduras or Panama, which are nearby and notably poorer. Similarly, economic need alone fails to explain why Taiwan, Korea, and India have been steady sources of migrants when other, less developed Asian nations have not. Simple poverty does not explain why skilled workers and middle-class entrepreneurs make up such a large part of the flow from countries as diverse as Colombia, Jamaica, India, and the Philippines.

One cannot simply look at the world, find poor people, and conclude that they are potential migrants. Indeed, even looking at a single country, it is incorrect to assume that the poorest regions will produce the greatest migrants. But there are recognizable patterns that reflect the evolving relationships between sending and receiving communities.

For example, four Mexican states produced more than half of the 1.6 million former illegal migrants who applied in California for the 1986 amnesty, and this massive human outflow came from a few highly concentrated sources within those states.[3] These were by no means the poorest nor the most crowded nor the most chaotic areas of Mexico. Instead, the migrants came from places that had long-standing traditions of sending people north. Some sent young men to work as *braceros* on the same farms year after year. In other cases whole branches of families had established themselves in the United States, and people moved back and forth between relatives here and relatives in Mexico as conditions warranted. But in almost every case, migration patterns developed over generations and often linked specific families or villages with specific destinations in the United States.[4]

THE SAFETY VALVE AND PUSH-PULL MODELS

The dynamic relationship between sending and receiving communities is often neglected in views of migration that focus only on economic factors, as with the oft-cited view that migration is a "safety valve" that relieves the pressures on a nation when it cannot create jobs as fast as it is producing new workers.

A slightly more dynamic view emphasizes a combination of "push" and "pull" factors that encourages migrants to leave their homes on the one hand and that draws them into host countries on the other. According to this model, wage differentials and comparative unemployment rates should determine who migrates and where they go.

The safety valve and push-pull models suggest a very broad range of potential migrants from virtually every poor country in the world, a possibility that leaves a receiving nation little to do but prepare defenses against a Malthusian catastrophe. On the other hand, if flows are rather particular and specific, then the perils can be defined and policies tailored accordingly.

While economic necessity and perceptions of opportunity undoubtedly do play a role in migration, the safety valve and push-pull formulas suffer two major limitations. First, these models reduce the migrant's motivations to little more than an individual's desire for escape from hardship. Not only is this inaccurate in a great many cases, but also it focuses on a misleading unit of analysis. A growing body of literature on both the European and the current wave of immigration shows that migration is often more a group behavior than an individual undertaking. All along, migrants have operated as families or as households, with the benefits of the migration often flowing to people who never leave home.

Second, the purely economic models depict an entire migrant stream as a kind of commodity that is subject to the laws of supply and demand. This view renders the movement of people as an assortment of distinct transactions between push and pull factors. It depicts each migrant's travels as the result of discreet and immediate market forces that carry a person on a one-way trip from less favorable conditions to better ones.

The danger in this case is to focus on a misleading time frame. The history of the European migration and mounting evidence from the current one show that migrant flows swell and recede and build again over long periods of time. Often these shifts reflect momentum rather than immediate circumstances. This suggests that to understand a particular migrant flow we must consider an ever-changing mix of factors that are continually changing the character of the migration.

The following two chapters offer a more detailed examination of the role of family structures and the evolution of migratory patterns. Together, these factors suggest that migration cannot be successfully regulated by altering the immediate circumstances of the flow even if that involves substantial change in the economic or political conditions of the sending country. Instead, like a captain trying to halt a fully laden oil tanker in the middle of the sea, immigration policy must contend most of all with momentum.

CHAPTER 5

TRAVELING FOR A FAMILY

Why aren't very poor people the most likely to migrate? If not the poorest, then who does come?

Some answers emerge from several extensive surveys of Mexican migrants both in Mexico and in the United States. Examining different populations and using a variety of methods over the course of nearly thirty years, these surveys came up with some remarkably consistent results.[1]

Whether Mexican migrants leave from the cities or countryside, they tend to have high rates of employment before they leave, often in comparatively good jobs requiring some skills in the local context. Their schooling and earnings place them neither at the bottom nor at the top of their communities. Even people who join the migrant stream as illegal aliens share these characteristics, clearly indicating that they are not emerging from the most desperate sectors of society. Usually migrants have more education and more skilled occupations than their parents. Finally, migrants or their families have often moved at least once within Mexico, and it is likely someone in the household has previously traveled north to the United States in search of work.

This portrait of the Mexican migrant does not fit the popular myth or the political rhetoric that forges an inextricable link between migration and poverty, but it does help explain some of the most important patterns in the current wave of migration. People who have managed to pull themselves up even just a little are likely to have different motivations and expectations than those stuck at the very bottom of the social ladder.

Moreover the surveys show that migrants typically do not act alone when they make the decision to travel. Instead, they usually operate as part of an

35

extended network of relatives and friends. These family or community-based networks not only facilitate travel but also provide it with a purpose. Often the goal of an individual's migration is realized with money sent home in the form of remittances.

Understanding the operations of these networks helps explain not only who comes but also how they get here and their purposes in being here. Any policy that aims at tempering migration pressures must take these factors into account.

To understand why migrants must rely on their relatives and why the poorest people in sending communities simply cannot migrate at all, one need only consider a hurdle that all migrants have faced through the ages: the costs of travel.

Making a trip to southern California from central Mexico might not seem very expensive, but a series of surveys supervised by Wayne A. Cornelius, director of the Center for U.S.-Mexican Studies at the University of California, San Diego, found that in the 1980s the average person in a rural sending community had to spend the equivalent of five months' income to finance travel. Aside from transportation costs, these expenses often included the fees paid to a *coyote*, a smuggler who guides migrants on clandestine border crossings, and money to cover living expenses while the migrant looked for work. In addition, there were the wages lost until the migrant got to the United States and got a job.

For people living at a subsistence level of poverty that price is too high. When a family has no savings at all, saving money for five months to invest in a risky trip north seems more ludicrous than impossible.

Instead of the very poor, it is the people a few steps above poverty who are most likely to migrate. Yet the travel involves high costs for them as well, so economic status cannot be the sole factor used to identify potential immigrants.

THE WORKINGS OF NETWORKS

Clearly, the people most likely to migrate are the ones best able to improve their odds of success when so much is put at risk. The most effective way of minimizing the risks is by migrating within a network made up of immediate family, kinfolk, and hometown friends. That is one reason why migrant flows tend to be self-perpetuating. Families are the brokerage houses of migration. They raise capital and spread risk. They vouchsafe the investment's legitimacy, and when it produces a profit in the form of remittances sent home by the migrant, the family distributes dividends.

The Cornelius surveys found that more than 40 percent of all the residents in traditional Mexican sending communities, including children and infants, had migrated at least once, some legally and some illegally, and that most adults had made several trips. People about to set off for the United

States said consistently that having a job prearranged for them was the key factor in deciding whether or not to travel. In fact, they considered the guarantee of a job more important than having legal immigrant status, and overwhelming numbers of them said their guarantees of work came through family networks.

Among those people considering migration for the first time, the Cornelius surveys showed 91 percent aiming for destinations in the United States where relatives were already living, while 95 percent had hometown friends at their U.S. destinations. These connections often developed over a generation or more of regular migration by different members of a single household.[2]

Migration networks are by no means only a Mexican phenomenon. In an extensive anthropological study of migration from the Dominican Republic, Glenn Hendricks offered a detailed picture of a sending community to which he gave the fictional name "Aldea." Extensive migration, he wrote of the village, "has transformed it and the area around it from a self-contained and rustic rural community to one whose culture and social organization are more directly tied to New York than to Santo Domingo."[3]

Such powerful networks provide not only the means for migration but also a motive. While the myths of migration laud the bold individual striving alone to make a new life, in fact the immigrant's struggle is often even more noble because it is a struggle on behalf of others. Growing evidence shows that immigrants past and present make their journeys as part of a family strategy for coping with economic change. Policymakers must realize that the results of immigration are often measured not in the migrant's new land but in the home community that is left behind.

THE THEORY OF RELATIVE DEPRIVATION

A series of studies conducted since the mid-1980s by the World Bank has experimented with the notion that "relative deprivation" is more important than absolute income in explaining why people migrate. A great many surveys and econometric equations that focused on rural Mexico bolstered the thesis that people measure their well-being by comparing themselves to their neighbors. Therefore, one major impetus to migration is to improve a household's status relative to other households in its immediate surroundings. The goal of the migration is to raise money, and thereby raise the family's standing in its home community.[4]

This helps explain why migrants emerge not from the most abject households in a community but from those that have some realistic hope for advancement. What needs to be emphasized is that the advancement takes place in the migrant's home community and not in the new land.

The idea of relative deprivation has several important implications. On a purely individual level it offers an econometric explanation for what seems a bit of common sense—hopelessness rarely engenders dramatic actions. Rather, people take risks when they have some hope of success. Rising expectations are therefore at least as much a stimulus to migration as descending ones, and rising economies are as likely to produce migrants as ones in economic free-fall. Perhaps the likeliest source of migrants is an economy that has lifted living standards somewhat and then falls into a crisis. Rising expectations are a powerful motivator, but unfulfilled expectations may be even stronger.

Under the scenario that the migrant does leave home as part of a household economic strategy, and that the migrant's gains are measured mainly by what is contributed to the welfare of those who remain behind, migration should be viewed as one of the means to overcome, or rather to get around, the rigid impediments to economic and social mobility that characterize so many Third World nations.

It is important to bear in mind that the influence of relative deprivation declines with distance from the home community. The farther the migrants wander in emotional as well as physical space from their original homes and the longer they are away, the less these factors are likely to matter.

A migrant's motivations and purposes change over time. Migrants are likely to be most concerned about families soon after they leave, but if they stay abroad, they become progressively more concerned with their new lives and send less money home. This brings about the self-perpetuation of networks. As remittances decline, households must send out new migrants to make up for those who no longer set their goals in the context of their home communities.

SENDING MONEY HOME

Consider the travels of Esteban Espinoza, a wiry man twenty-five years old, who grew up on a *rancho*, or small farm, in the Mexican state of Guerrero, where his family raised mostly corn. In summer 1993, he found himself standing on the street corners near downtown Los Angeles that have become a well-known day labor market. During the course of the summer he painted houses, worked for a landscaper, and unloaded trucks at garment district warehouses. The pay was always close to the minimum wage, $4.25 an hour, and always in cash.

Esteban figured that he wired home between $150 to $200 a week. Housing was a blanket on the floor of a church-run shelter. All his belongings fit into a small gym bag. Every day he spent at least twelve hours working or looking for work.

"On Saturday I send back whatever I have and just keep $5 for myself and that is always enough until Monday or Tuesday and by then I've made some more," he said.

Eleven adults and children live on the *rancho*.

"We raise a lot of different kinds of food and usually we have enough to eat but there is never much money," Esteban explained. "With someone up here working, there is money every week."

One of Esteban's grandfathers picked chilies and did railroad work in the United States many years back, he recalled, and his father had gone north for a time as well. In the more recent past an elder brother was assigned to make the trip north to be the *rancho's* cash cow, but when he found a regular job he began staying in Los Angeles over the winters. Then he married, and gradually his remittances dropped off. The task fell to Esteban, who made two trips of a few weeks each in 1992 to visit his brother and to learn the business, including the tricks for crossing the border.

On his own now, Esteban expected to stay in Los Angeles until the rains came in the autumn. Then he planned to go back to the *rancho*. "In the winter I will rest, and in the spring I will probably come back, and then I will find a real place to live, and real work, and maybe I will stay for a year."

Asked whether he would ever consider staying permanently in California the way his brother did, Esteban breaks a bit of a smile and says, "It depends on the future." As powerful as his links to the *rancho* might have been at the moment, Esteban clearly did not consider them permanent.

Money sent home by people like Esteban is part of a massive and growing transfer of funds. This financial traffic is the most tangible supporting evidence for the idea that migration finds its fulfillment in economic strategies played out in the countries of origin.

According to World Bank estimates, the total value of remittances from migrants worldwide increased from $43.3 billion in 1980 to $65.5 billion in 1989. By 1993 the total was rapidly approaching $70 billion, despite the effects of a long recession in most industrialized economies, according to a United Nations estimate. This means the money scrimped and saved and sent home by migrants amounted to the second-largest form of international monetary flow in the world, coming in behind the oil trade ($240 billion in total exports in 1984) but well ahead of the next-largest commodity, coffee ($9 billion on average in the early 1980s).[5]

Remittances just from Mexican workers in the United States amounted to an estimated $3.2 billion in 1990. That is a fairly conservative figure, considering that some calculations go as high as $6 billion. But even at this level, remittances would easily exceed Mexico's annual income from agricultural exports ($2.2 billion) and the value of foreign direct investment in the country ($2.6 billion).[6]

According to various estimates, something like 20 to 25 percent of the entire Mexican population benefits from remittances, with the figure going as high as two-thirds or more of the population in traditional rural sending communities.[7]

The financial link between migrants and their home communities is not by any means a particularly Latin trait. Nations such as Jordan and Egypt are just as dependent on remittances as is Mexico. Nor is this massive dispatch of funds something new.

During the second half of nineteenth century, annual remittances from Irish migrants in the United States exceeded $8 million in some years. Considering those sums, Patrick J. Blessing concluded that the "large-scale Irish peasant movement to the New World, therefore, was not a mindless flight from intolerable conditions, but, within the limited range of alternatives, a deliberate departure of generally literate individuals who were very much concerned with the survival and well-being of family and friends remaining at home."[8]

The functioning of household networks need not always be so altruistic, however. In a compelling new analysis of contemporary migration from the Dominican Republic to New York City, Sherri Grasmuck and Patricia R. Pessar argue that households do not always send out migrants as part of a collective economic strategy. They describe how in many patriarchal households some sons find an escape in migration, while others are forced to leave because they are less favored than their brothers. Such departures are especially common when a household switches its land use to commercial agriculture, begins to employ wage laborers, and renders some family members into excess labor. Grasmuck and Pessar also present compelling accounts of how migration has become a means for many women to escape restrictive domestic ideologies and to experience the liberating power of becoming a breadwinner.[9]

So people leave to get away from family arrangements as well as to help support them. Indeed, given the nature of the human spirit and the powerful motivating force of guilt, it is perfectly plausible for a single migrant to embrace both goals: to seek escape from a traditional household arrangement and then to send large quantities of money home as a form of penance.

If this view of the migrant as a participant in an extended household network is valid for Ireland circa 1890, Mexico in the 1980s, and the Dominican Republic in the 1990s, then it must have some broad implications. To the extent that it helps explain who comes and why, it should be an important factor in crafting policies aimed at reducing migration pressures. Moreover, an understanding of migrants' links to their home countries should inform policies governing their presence here, including their place in the labor force.

But no matter how important they are to the dynamics of migration, household networks are only vehicles. At best they can offer only clues to the forces that fuel migration and control its directions.

CHAPTER 6

TRAVELING THE CHANNELS

A stream of Irish immigrants has been coming to the United States almost without interruption for more than three hundred years.

In the 1690s the colonial governments of South Carolina, Maryland, and Virginia all passed laws aimed at limiting immigration by Irish Catholic servants. Three centuries later, and thirty years after the election of the first president of Irish descent, Irish Americans persuaded Congress to ease the rules for immigration from Ireland. Droves of young people had evaded restrictive regulations by coming illegally, and therefore could find work only as waiters, bartenders, and nannies. Yet the Irish migration actually peaked in the middle of this chronology, when the potato famine sent nearly 1.5 million Irish immigrants across the Atlantic in the 1840s and early 1850s.

The history of this migrant stream is exceptional only in its duration. It teaches us that human migrations can develop as the unintended byproduct of the relationships between nations and that the migrant flow can become well established despite official efforts in the country of destination to resist it.

The Irish case shows that once a channel is established it takes on a life of its own, drawing people from different sectors of the nation at different times. The impulse to migrate rolls through a society in response to a variety of political and economic events. Emigration from Ireland was prompted by increasing demand for grains during the Napoleonic Wars, then by the potato famine, the mechanization of agriculture, and even by the improvement of roadways, which permitted the efficient delivery of British manufactured goods to small towns in the late nineteenth century.

This history tells us that a migration can begin for one reason, as a response to a given historical moment, and then reach its peak under an entirely different set of circumstances in a different epoch altogether. This history also proves that such developments can occur in cycles. Once a migratory channel is established, it provides an ongoing, readily available outlet for people responding to the crisis of the moment.

In sum, the history of immigration from Ireland to the United States demonstrates how a migratory channel can become a permanent and influential link between two societies. It shows how the human traffic on that channel evolves over time, assuming novel forms that build on the past but are constantly adapting to a changing present.

Many of these lessons can be generalized and applied to contemporary immigration to the United States from Latin America. The 1990 census counted 4.3 million Mexican-born people living in the United States. They, too, represent the results of migratory channels that have been evolving across generations, as did the 737,000 U.S. residents and citizens who were born in Cuba or the 348,000 who were born in the Dominican Republic.

The balance of this chapter will identify some universal characteristics of migratory channels, and the following chapter will examine the dynamics of the most important contemporary migration to the United States, the influx from Mexico. An understanding of how a migration evolves through several stages is essential to the making of any long-term policy.

How, then, can we mark the stages in the evolution of migratory channels? How can we generalize about the course that migrations take over long periods of time?

Saskia Sassen, professor of Urban Planning at Columbia University, defines two important stages of a migration in her pioneering work, *The Mobility of Labor and Capital.* She suggests drawing a distinction between the *beginning* of a new migration flow and its *continuation.*[1]

She argues that the beginning of a migration involves factors in both the sending and receiving countries that allow for "the formation of objective and subjective linkages . . . that make such migration feasible."

Migrants are bold souls, and the United States is a powerful magnet. Yet migration almost always follows preexisting channels that can develop in many ways, often inadvertently and often at the instigation of the United States. These channels represent more than just migration routes. In many ways, they are the sum of all the objective and subjective linkages between two nations.

THE STAGES OF MIGRATION: BEGINNING

Migratory channels often develop slowly, upon a basis of a limited and very specific movement of peoples, before eventually blossoming into something much more generalized. Moreover, the linkages between two countries begin and take on their own character years, even decades before a wave of migrants begins to leave home. In the cases of both the Dominican Republic and Nicaragua, the linkage was initially forged by way of military intervention and was then reinforced by trade, investment, popular culture, and a weighty diplomatic influence. Korea, Vietnam, and the Philippines also fit the model whereby military action marks the first step toward creating a migratory channel.

But soldiers are by no means necessary to start a migration. All across Latin America the pervasiveness of U.S. economic and cultural influences has created a familiarity among peoples, a psychic closeness, that eases the creation of migratory channels.

In all of these cases, from Seoul to Santo Domingo, the United States reached out and touched another country in a way that established a link between them. Later, when economic conditions in both the sending and receiving countries fell into the right configuration of supply and demand, a mass migration resulted.

THE STAGES OF MIGRATION: CONTINUATION

In Sassen's view the next stage in a migration, the continuation, largely reflects the host country's demand for immigrant labor. However, two other factors also tend to promote migration at this point, and during the current wave of migration to the United States these factors are profoundly intertwined: government policies and the functioning of family networks.

Since it was adopted in 1965, the U.S. policy of family-based immigration has had a profound long-term effect in maintaining immigration. The preference given by law to family reunification often makes the family a more powerful force than the economy in determining migration levels. Until the 1960s, migratory flows to the United States diminished sharply and almost automatically in response to economic downturns, but this effect has been significantly blunted by family reunification. Aside from the fact that familial ties rather than gain becomes a major motivating force, the law itself frequently obliges people to spend years waiting for a visa, so that migration cannot be timed to economic cycles.

Applying Sassen's framework to the Irish case, one sees that the historical relationship between Ireland and England fostered the emergence of a migratory channel to Britain's American colonies in the seventeenth century. Rising demand for low-wage laborers in U.S. cities helped perpetuate this flow during the second half of the nineteenth century. But this tells only part of the story and fails to account for events like the mass migration during the potato famine or the long periods when immigration from Ireland dropped off significantly.

The Stages of Migration: Explosion and Diminution

At least two other stages of migration also deserve attention.

Besides the beginning and the continuation of a migrant flow, there is also often a moment of *explosion*. In many cases migrations go on for decades at a steady pace and then suddenly the numbers shoot up drastically. This happened to Ireland during the Great Famine and then again in the 1880s, when thousands of people lost their livelihoods to technological change and new patterns of international trade. These two very different events produced similar results in the migratory flow (see Figure 6.1).

During the current wave of immigration to the United States, explosive migrations have come from Cuba, Haiti, Mexico, the Dominican Republic, and the Philippines. In all these cases, ongoing migrations have spiked suddenly at different times and for different reasons.

Figure 6.1
Irish Immigration
Totals by Decades

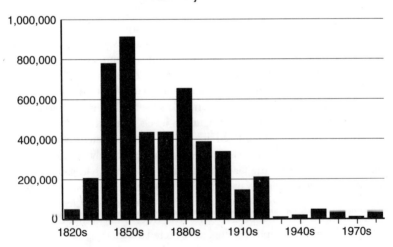

Source: U.S. Department of Justice, *Statistical Yearbook of the Immigration and Naturalization Service*, 1992.

Finally, there is the stage of *diminution*, when the numbers drop off over a period of time. Sometimes this denotes nothing more than a temporary slump, with a strong flow rekindling some years later. Other times there is a real hiatus, and when the migration resumes it takes on a new form. And there is always the possibility of a final and complete halt to the movement.

The conditions that produce an explosive migration are especially important to understand because it is the sudden and substantial increase in a flow that most often raises immigration to the level of a crisis for policymakers. Often a single spectacular event can push much broader immigration issues onto the national agenda.

For example, the 1980 Mariel "boatlift" from Cuba produced very dramatic television pictures but only about 130,000 migrants, less than 1 percent of all those who have come during the current wave of immigration. However, the crowded fishing boats became a symbol for a nation seemingly at the mercy of events. Ronald Reagan excoriated Jimmy Carter on this theme in the presidential election that year, and subsequently Mariel helped set the political context that eventually produced the immigration reform law of 1986.

THE RISKS OF A NEW EXPLOSION

Today, many politicians, advocates, and academics are warning that immigration could easily spin out of control again. This generalized anxiety sees the threat of massive inflows emerging from causes as varied as sub-Saharan desertification and ethnic strife in Tajikistan. However, if history offers any help in judging the risks of explosive migration, one can safely argue that vast numbers of migrants do not simply appear on our doorsteps out of nowhere.

Even at moments of massive and seemingly chaotic movement, migration tends to follow preexisting channels. For example, the migratory path from Ireland to the United States was well established much before the Great Famine, so when catastrophe hit, migration was a readily available outlet and the numbers of people traveling exploded. Similarly, the Mariel exodus from Cuba in 1980 reflected conditions on the island and resulted from specific events there. But it could have only happened because anti-Castro Cubans were already well established so nearby in Miami, and even the migration that began in 1959 followed a path that had linked Cuba to Florida for five hundred years.[2]

Great migrations that have failed to materialize in the United States make the same point. Brazil and Venezuela have gone through periods of economic crises that could have prompted notable migrations northward but did not. Argentina through much of the 1970s experienced both economic and political upheaval without throwing off migrants to the United States. What was missing in all of these cases was the right kind of connection to the United States.

Once the linkages are formed, a small migration can continue for decades almost unnoticed. Then, when an economic, political, military, or natural catastrophe strikes the sending country, migration has become a ready option for displaced people. Suddenly, often quite unexpectedly, the receiving country finds itself subject to an explosive migration with major consequences.

Nowhere is this pattern of evolution more evident today than in the migration of several million Mexicans to southern California beginning in the early 1980s. This was the most striking contemporary example of an existing migratory channel suddenly blossoming into an explosive flow. But the migration of Mexicans to the United States is also the longest, largest, most continuous international migration currently under way anywhere in the world.

CHAPTER 7

THE MEXICAN CASE

On any given night, especially in the spring and summer, people dart furtively under, around, and over the fence that divides Tijuana from the sprawling southern suburbs of San Diego. Frequent repetition by the news media has imbedded this scene in the public's consciousness as a symbol of Mexican immigration. Sometimes this scene stands as a symbol for all contemporary migration, a symbol that readily inspires phrases like "clamor at the gates," "flood of illegals," "Mexican invasion," and that touchstone of immigration crisis, "Our borders are out of control."

The power of these images and phrases is such that policymakers are often tempted to view illegal immigration as an emergency that can be subjected to immediate cures, such as a better fence or a more effective Border Patrol. The unprecedented and largely uncontrolled influx of illegal immigrants from Mexico is indeed one of the defining characteristics of contemporary immigration, but it is hardly an immediate development. Instead, it is the product of a long evolution that has progressed in stages, as described in the previous chapter. The search for an effective policy response has to begin with an understanding of that evolution.

BUILDING THE CHANNEL

The linkage between the two countries was established in the mid-nineteenth century when Mexico became an object of American territorial expansion, but it was a long time before this link developed into a migratory channel.

By 1900, for example, the original *Californios*, the Mexican ranchers who had settled the West Coast, had all but disappeared, and in Los Angeles people of Mexican descent accounted for only 15 percent of the total population.

Then came the first in a clear sequence of events that culminated in the crowds at the Tijuana fence almost a century later. At the beginning of this century, the Santa Fe and the Southern Pacific railroads extended their lines deep into Mexico, recruiting workers as they laid track. Meanwhile, the dictator Porfirio Diaz invited foreign investment, which transformed the economy. Inflation and industrialization drove people to migrate. The railroads not only offered jobs in the north, they also formed an iron conduit to Los Angeles, where one of the first twentieth-century barrios sprang up across the river from the railyards. For the next two decades the border was basically left open.

By 1910 a migrant channel had been established between California and central Mexico, with the northern states often serving as a jumping-off point.

In 1911 a congressional report on immigration by a body known as the Dillingham Commission concluded, "In the case of the Mexican, he is less desirable as a citizen than as a laborer."

Between 1910 and 1920, the Mexican Revolution produced the first bout of explosive migration, as chaos in Mexico coincided with an economic boom in southern California. The state's growers became so dependent on Mexican workers that they convinced Congress to exempt Mexican immigrants from the literacy test required of immigrants after 1917.

Mexicans were exempted again when Washington adopted the national quota laws of the 1920s. As a result, Mexican workers swept into industrial jobs when the supply of new labor from southern Europe dried up. In the 1920s, the influx from Mexico more than doubled even as immigration from Europe fell to less than half of what it had been. Then in 1942 Washington instituted what was a temporary wartime program of allowing Mexican contract laborers, or *braceros*, into the country for six months at a time. At the behest of agricultural interests in California and the Southwest, the program was extended until 1964. Eventually more than four million Mexicans got to know the way north working as *braceros*. In 1952 the so-called Texas Proviso to the McCarran-Walter Act specifically exempted the employment of illegal aliens from any penalty.

Mexican immigrants were treated like a commodity not only when the economy was growing but also when it shrank. Just as the government invited them in during the good times, it conducted massive deportations in the 1930s and again in the 1950s, when the Mexican workers were judged superfluous during economic downturns.

By the 1960s the migratory channel had become deeply imbedded in both California and Mexico. But political change in the United States eliminated the tools by which traffic on that channel was regulated. After the *bracero* program was brought to an end, much of the same migratory traffic continued on an illegal basis. But in the atmosphere of the civil rights era, mass deportations became unthinkable.[1]

Simultaneously, the Vietnam War produced a boom in southern California and many of the migrants who had previously worked the fields of the Central Valley moved into the bustling Los Angeles labor market. This redirection of the flow picked up again in the late 1970s, when manufacturing jobs in California increased at four times the national average. In the early 1980s, recent Mexican immigrants were more than three times as likely to hold low-skilled manufacturing jobs as non-Hispanic whites.[2]

At this point everything was set for a migration comparable in size and suddenness only to the one that followed the Irish potato famine. The transportation routes were familiar and well worn. Robust receiving communities were in place to ease the newcomers' adjustment to the United States. Mexican migrants were well established in several different niches of the labor force, from construction to food service.

THE EXPLOSION OF THE 1980S

Between 1981 and 1992 immigration to California exploded, as the state gained some 1.5 million legal Mexican immigrants.[3] In addition, between half a million and a million Mexicans who had crossed the border illegally lived in the state more or less permanently at different times during this period, and there was a constant and very sizable flow of Mexicans who migrated to California to work there temporarily. So large and concentrated an influx of migrants was unprecedented in U.S. history.

But human events of such size do not take place for no reason. Three conditions had to be in place for this migratory explosion to take place:

- A well-established migratory channel, to provide the means

- The 1980s economic boom in California—the nation's longest, fastest, and richest peacetime economic expansion—to provide the opportunity

- Mexico's devastating economic crisis, to provide the motive

Mexico's crisis was extreme. After the collapse of oil prices in 1982, external debt increased almost tenfold by 1987, to $107 billion. Through much of the 1980s, interest payments alone ate up half the value of the nation's exports.

As a result of the crushing debt and declining income, the government held down wages, slashed social programs, and allowed prices to rise. These decisions, combined with the effects of capital flight from the private sector, produced an overall 15 percent drop in per capita income at the height of the crisis, from 1982 to 1988. By several measures the number of people living in poverty doubled, as did underemployment.

Absent this economic catastrophe, Mexican immigration would not have increased so rapidly from the mid-1980s to the early 1990s. The pattern of migration that was established in the early part of the century had been on the rise in one form or another for decades, and surely it would have continued to increase in the 1980s. But the oil crisis generated an acceleration in migration much more drastic than could have been predicted.

Perhaps it was an episode. Now that Mexico's economy is on the mend and California's is stuck in a painful period of restructuring, the factors that caused and sustained that explosion are receding. Indeed, several different studies indicate that the flow of people into California diminished in 1992 and 1993. Overall, the underlying rate of legal Mexican migration is now close to what it averaged in the 1970s, if one excludes the ongoing legalization of amnesty applicants who arrived in the United States years ago. Migration rates, however, sometimes take several years to respond to events, and given the unknown size of the illegal flow it is difficult to know exactly where things stand. It is possible, though, that the numbers have hit a plateau.

THE EXPLOSION'S LONG AFTERMATH

What happened in the 1980s between Mexico and California increasingly appears to fit the well-established historical model of a migratory flow that explodes in response to specific circumstances and then recedes when those circumstances no longer prevail. This does not mean, however, that Mexican immigration is going to stop. It has gone on for nearly a century and has developed its own internal momentum. Moreover, the 1980s explosion created new migratory channels and new family relationships that will in turn lead to decades of further migration.

The Mexican immigration of the 1980s was in many ways different from those of earlier decades. Many more women and complete families came north than before, and these groups tended to settle down more than the individual male migrants of the past. The influx of the 1980s also included sectors of Mexican society that had not participated heavily in past migrations.[4]

The U.S. government may be the most important influence in ensuring that migration continues long into the future. The more than two million formerly illegal migrants from Mexico who benefited from the 1986 amnesty are now becoming eligible for U.S. citizenship. Those who chose to naturalize themselves will gain the right to sponsor relatives as legal immigrants.

The possibility that immigration from Mexico has at least temporarily reached a plateau, or has even begun to decline, has major consequences for how the United States will design its immigration policies for the rest of the 1990s. The spike in Mexican migration during the 1980s accounted for more than 35 percent of the legal entries to the United States, and the Mexican share of illegal arrivals was even greater. Even a small decline in the rate of Mexican migration would have a major impact on the overall immigration picture for the 1990s.

Mexico is undergoing a process of social, political, and economic change that is full of uncertainties. The New Year's uprising in the state of Chiapas was symptomatic of the tensions that arise from so much flux. The movement of people to the United States is another symptom.

Migration between the United States and Mexico has become so deeply ingrained in the life of both societies that movement north is no mere byproduct of change. Migration is not only an effect of change in Mexico, but it is also a cause of change. It strongly influences Mexico's contemporary history, serving as a source of revenue by way of remittances, an outlet for frustration, a source of cultural influences, and a major determinant of the labor-force structure.

Though immigration from Mexico seems certain to continue at rates high enough to have a substantial impact on the United States, at this point there is no reason to assume immigration will continue at levels reached in the early 1990s. Nor is there any reason to predict another sudden and massive increase in migration anytime soon. Even in the absence of an explosive migration from Mexico, however, the United States clearly has a long-term interest in trying to manage the human flow.

CHAPTER 8

TOWARD A POLICY OF ENTRY

M exico generated the largest but by no means the only migration flow
that surged in the 1980s. Almost every part of the world except for sub-
Saharan Africa produced an increased flow of immigrants to the United States
since the current wave of migration began. But as with Mexico, there is reason
to hope that flows from several other sending countries have also crested.

Legal immigration from Central America nearly quadrupled in the 1980s.
The largest increase came from El Salvador, where the flow of legal immigrants to the United States rose from some 34,000 in the 1970s to nearly
214,000 in the 1980s. The major reason for the explosion in migration from
Central America in the 1980s lay in the civil wars that bloodied almost the
entire region during that decade. For the most part those wars are now over.
Family reunification policies in the United States assure a continuing flow of
immigrants from those countries, but the explosive moment has passed and the
numbers already show signs of coming down.

A survey of the major sources of migration going into the mid-1990s
indicates that the overall numbers for this decade may not be significantly
higher than in the 1980s. There is some chance the numbers might even be
somewhat lower, especially from Latin America.

If this forecast holds true, policymakers already face a distinctly different
set of circumstances than those they faced in the late 1980s. When migrations are surging, a receiving country has few good options; as the numbers
wane, opportunities to reduce migration pressures in the long run multiply.

In almost every case, initiatives to eliminate the causes of an explosive migration before it occurs are likely to win support in both the sending and receiving nations. Conversely, almost every action aimed at cutting off a burst of migration once it has begun is likely to be controversial, and probably ineffective.

There are three areas in which the United States could take the initiative:

- Establishing models of economic development that aim at reducing migration pressures and specifically take into account the role that family networks play in promoting and maintaining migratory flows

- Placing immigration at the center of bilateral relations with nations that have well-established migratory channels to the United States

- Attempting to preempt explosive migrations whenever they appear to be developing

This third option amounts to little more than emergency-room care. Obviously, resources would be more efficiently used in the first two proposals, which can be thought of respectively as preventive medicine and an attempt to manage a chronic condition.

MIGRATION AND DEVELOPMENT POLICIES

The most difficult of these three initiatives would be to formulate development policies with migration outcomes in mind. This has not been tried very much before, and it involves a great many unknowns.

The depth of uncertainty was clearly evident during the debate over the North American Free Trade Agreement (NAFTA). Some experts argued that greater trade with the United States would cut migration from Mexico, but equally impressive arguments suggested that the flows would increase. The consensus seemed to be that migration would increase for ten to twenty years and then drop off.

Until now, managing migration pressures has received scant attention in the formation of development policies, either in the context of bilateral aid or multilateral institutions. Indeed, many successful development projects have as an unintended consequence stimulated migration. These include the commercialization of agriculture to produce export crops, the concentration of industries in megacities, and the creation of high-turnover job structures. Whenever the United States promotes these forms of development, it clearly has an interest in examining the potential for increasing migration. This is especially important if it has an active migration channel with the nation in question.

For example, immigration was only a latent issue during the negotiation of NAFTA, but it should be a constant and explicit consideration in its implementation. Reducing tariff barriers on the least competitive sectors of the Mexican economy with too much haste will leave Mexico exposed to a sudden influx of cheaper, U.S.-made goods. The result will be an equally sudden surge in migration, as displaced workers head north.

Efforts could also be made to direct U.S. investment to areas of Mexico that have produced large emigrations. Such an initiative would have to be engineered to enhance the reasons why a Mexican would want to stay in those regions over the long term. This rules out the kind of low-wage, high-turnover employment that characterizes most U.S.-owned assembly plants along the border; a form of economic development that might even lead in the long term to increased migration.

Mexico and the United States might try to work out a plan to make more productive use of remittances. Today, those funds often help sustain otherwise uneconomic forms of household activity, such as marginal farming, or they go to the construction of second homes for people living in the United States who vacation or retire in Mexico. Conceivably the Mexican government could help create opportunities for more productive investment of such funds, while the United States could help create a low-cost and secure means for migrants to transfer those funds home.

The result would be something like a binational community bank. The money would stay within an extended household network, but the institution would encourage the most effective use of the funds. Perhaps such a remittance bank would help the migrant's family put the funds sent home into a productive investment. The goal would be to help migration fulfill its purposes and thereby end the sending communities' economic dependence on a constant flow of new migrants.

No easy answers are readily apparent, and any initiatives of this sort may provoke all sorts of unintended consequences. But it is clear the time has come to find more innovative ways to address the problem. Successful development has until now often been measured with cold mathematics. Increased gross domestic product, increased trade flows, and increased productivity are all considered marks of success regardless of how many people are displaced along the way.

In an era of mass migration, a decreased outflow of people should be a measure of development success, so long as that decrease means that a greater number of people are happy to stay home. Both the United States and the nations of the developing world share an interest in that outcome.

MIGRATION DIPLOMACY

The management of migration pressures should assume a central place not just in development policies but in all aspects of relations with countries linked to the United States by an active migration channel.

An active and strong migration constitutes a special relationship between any two countries, with advantages and disadvantages for both parties. No less than political, economic, or military ties, this migration relationship needs the attention of policymakers.

The most obvious place for such a policy to focus would be in Mexico. Both Mexico and the United States would have to give up certain pretenses to sovereignty that have kept them from effectively addressing what is by far the most important aspect of their bilateral relations. As the larger nation, and the one with the most to lose in any large, uncontrolled immigration, the United States should take the initiative.

Already, the Clinton administration has offered to discuss in advance any changes in border policy, such as the erection of fences or changes in procedure by the Border Patrol or Customs. In exchange, the Mexicans might agree to cooperate with simple measures, such as ordering their police to stop smugglers seen digging holes under the border fence in broad daylight. They might also prevent large crowds of people from amassing on the Mexican side of the fence for an illegal rush across the border, a technique often used to overwhelm the Border Patrol.

Though such initiatives may seem simple, they would require major changes in hard and often hostile attitudes on both sides of the border. They would, one could hope, stand as a prelude to a much more serious discussion of the vast human traffic between the two nations.

With the end of the Cold War, the United States can redefine its interests in many parts of the world. In Central America, if there is no threat of a Communist-supported insurgency, U.S. national interests can now be defined in terms of managing migration. Active encouragement of political reconciliation, economic aid, and continuous pressure on human rights are not merely matters of altruism or a naive democratic idealism. Instead, U.S. involvement and expenditures in Central America can now be justified as opportunities to prevent explosive migrations in the future, and on this basis such policies might garner widespread support.

Haiti, unfortunately, has rapidly become an example of how such opportunities can be lost. The United States has virtually no national interest in Haiti, except to prevent the sudden and uninvited appearance of Haitians on Florida beaches. While it might seem cynical, the one basis on which an aggressive and consistent policy toward Haiti might find broad domestic support is as a means to control migration.

During the seven months President Jean-Bertrand Aristide held office, migration dropped. An emphasis on migration priorities would have led the United States to give him greater support, even though some in Washington considered him a leftist firebrand. Such support might have preempted his ouster by the military in 1991 and the explosive outflow of boat people that followed the military takeover.

A desire to end the migration crisis was the unspoken assumption behind the cheering when the Governors Island Agreements were signed July 3, 1993. Those accords called for the removal of the military regime and Aristide's restoration as Haiti's democratically elected president. If migration control had been an explicit and emphasized aspect of U.S. policy, the Clinton administration might have been less reluctant to take decisive action when implementation of the accords faltered in autumn 1993.

By early 1994 increased repression by the military government and the ongoing economic crisis in Haiti had built up pressures for another explosive migration. The Clinton administration found itself obliged to discourage Haitians from fleeing even as it denounced their oppressors.

An unraveling of the peace process in either El Salvador or Nicaragua would put the United States in a similar bind. The lesson to be drawn from Haiti is that the United States cannot walk away from foreign policy failures involving countries that are main sources of migrants. The consequences will soon come right home.

PREEMPTING EXPLOSIONS

The third area where initiatives can be taken—attempting to preempt explosive migrations—is closely related to the management of migratory channels.

The United States has a clear self-interest in preventing itself from becoming the destination of large, sudden, and uncontrolled migrations. This point would seem obvious, but in the past no great effort has been made to forecast or prevent such situations.

For example, would the Reagan administration have adopted different policies toward the rescheduling of Mexico's external debt if policymakers had thought there was a chance that doing so would cut the influx of Mexican immigrants by half?

Looking toward the future, there is one nation that demands special attention as the potential source of an explosive migration: Cuba.

It seems safe to say that no matter how the Castro regime comes to an end, and the laws of nature require him to die some day, there is likely to be a sudden and massive influx of Cubans across the Straits of Florida. As conditions on the island deteriorate, the size of a potential post-Castro migration grows exponentially. No matter what the political future holds, the economic situation alone ensures that huge numbers of people will want to leave. Unless the next regime is even more effective than the current one in keeping people from departing, there will be an exodus. The Cubans of Miami will be in Havana harbor with their own boats to ensure that it happens. If the island is beset by political chaos and/or violence, such a migration could easily bring along a few hundred thousand people, dwarfing the size of the 1980 Mariel boatlift.

In other words, Castro's demise is virtually certain to bring about a prolonged crisis, with the greatest challenges for U.S. policymakers developing in Florida rather than in Cuba.

These dire possibilities argue for a complete reorientation of policy toward Cuba. The Castro regime no longer exports its revolution to the rest of Latin America, but it threatens an invasion of Florida. Indeed, the prospect of Castro's demise must again make Cuba a major foreign policy concern, and the danger of a catastrophic migration needs to become the top priority. Unfortunately, the United States has relatively few means with which to influence the situation.

Turning away Cuban refugees after more than thirty years of welcoming them seems cruel as well as politically untenable. But U.S. law does offer the option of "temporary protected status," which embraces the classic notion of refuge as a temporary asylum rather than a permanent home. Such a concept is workable if the status really is temporary rather than a prolonged limbo. Fleeing Cubans would be granted admission only until a government formally recognized by the United States took power in Havana, and the assistance offered by the federal government would be in the form of temporary shelter rather than resettlement. An obvious exception would be made for those qualifying for regular immigration status as relatives of people already here.

Such a policy change cannot be implemented after an exodus has begun. Instead, it has to be designed and announced well in advance so as to shape perceptions and expectations.

As for the Castro regime, U.S. policy will always be hostile to it and will aim at bringing about its end. But if migration is regarded as a major concern, then the United States may not have any real interest in running Cuba's economy any further into the ground with its complete trade embargo. Worsening conditions on the island may or may nor hasten the end of Castro's rule, but they will certainly increase the size of the migration after he falls and prolong the duration of an exodus once it has begun.

This is not to suggest that the embargo can immediately be lifted or even modified. Such a proposal at present has no chance of acceptance in Washington. The embargo seems to be a fixture on the international scene. But recently such fixtures have had a habit of becoming unfixed. Dealing with Castro is as much of an anathema as dealing with Yasir Arafat was just a few years ago. Migration interests require a discussion of the possibility of change in the diplomatic landscape.

If current conditions prevail, Washington should prepare for a massive uncontrolled migration from Cuba. This will have enormous political and economic impact in the United States, especially in Florida, because it will happen very quickly and very dramatically. In response, virtually the only thing that federal authorities will be able to do is to ensure the safety of the high seas and to write checks. Local authorities will demand, and have every right to expect, immediate federal aid in accommodating the refugees. Congress, the administration, and the federal bureaucracy should have no doubt that Washington will bear total financial responsibility for the domestic consequences of Castro's demise, and it will be a very expensive proposition.

That is the bad news, but there is not much of it and that is the good news.

Of all immigration threats, only Cuba has the potential to create an immediate and uncontrolled migration measured in the hundreds of thousands. And while such an event would have a major political impact, as a demographic matter it would be small compared to the Mexican immigration of the 1980s. It would be a stretch of the imagination to come up with any scenario for a migration explosion that does not involve Mexico and that could still land a million or more people in the United States in the course of a decade.

Western Europe faces a much more difficult future. It is already absorbing refugees from the warfare in the former Yugoslavia, and it will continue to do so for a long time. But the worst may be yet to come.

Egypt and Algeria top the list of nations living under the threat of an Islamic fundamentalist revolution. A bloody uprising anywhere in North Africa, let alone a successful takeover, would spark an enormous exodus across the Mediterranean.

Migrant streams from sub-Saharan Africa have already established themselves in several Western European countries, raising the possibility of explosive migrations in response to environmental or economic catastrophes. And from Siberia to Slovakia, the whole of the former Soviet bloc has the potential of generating sudden migrations. Not only does Europe face a multitude of dangers, but each of those dangers involves large populations only a short distance away, sometimes just across land borders.

Common concern over migration among the United States and its longtime allies raises the possibility of concerted, common efforts to address this issue. Although not the strategic threat that Communism once was, mass migration threatens enough disruption that it merits action in a multilateral context.

What direction might such action take?

The Clinton administration should have no trouble finding an answer. Its own commissioner of the Immigration and Naturalization Service, Doris Meissner, laid out an approach in article published by *Foreign Policy* in spring 1992, when she was director of the immigration policy program at the Carnegie

Endowment. Her formulation is so well articulated that it deserves to be quoted at length:

> During the Cold War, the right of individuals to leave communist societies became a cornerstone of the Helsinki process and an emblem of democratic values. This principle must now be recast to underscore its corollary: the right to stay. Most people prefer their home countries and will stay if conditions are barely tolerable. It is that impulse that policy must build on. The human rights principle of freedom of movement should reflect options and choice, not necessity. An international ethos anchored in the right to stay would devote unswerving attention to strengthening respect for human rights, supporting economic policies that emphasize jobs and better living standards, and preventing conflicts that spawn destabilizing migrations.[1]

The United States will have to exercise care in managing these flows and taking measures to prevent explosive migrations when possible. The right to stay could serve as a guiding principle that brings migration into the center of post-Cold War foreign policy. But managing migration flows deals only with one aspect of immigration—entry.

The ongoing challenges now lie in the cities of the United States, not on its borders. This country is now on the receiving end of mature and robust migratory flows. It already has a large immigrant population, and that population is certain to grow for years to come. The time has come to shift emphasis from who comes to what happens to immigrants once they are here. The real issue of the 1990s will be integration rather than entry.

III

INTEGRATION: A DOMESTIC AFFAIR

CHAPTER 9

BEYOND THE MELTING POT
AND THE MOSAIC

After moving to Houston from Mexico when she was three years old, Imelda grew up in a household fractured by competing identities.

Her parents' world was circumscribed by the factories where they worked by day, their nighttime jobs cleaning offices, and the little bit of the barrio they saw during their rare hours off. The American city, with all its complexities and conflicts, was just a downtown skyline visible on clear days in the distance. After a dozen years the parents spoke all the English they needed to get by, which wasn't much.

Imelda learned English from the television, her constant childhood companion and window into the country she now considered home. In the working-class neighborhood where she grew up, Imelda barely kept one step ahead of the gangs and drugs and violence that were consuming whole sections of the Sun Belt city. Almost by instinct, Imelda seemed streetwise and sassy.

By the time she reached high school, Imelda's world had begun to clash with that of her parents.

"We could never get stuff like pizza at home, just Mexican foods," Imelda said not long after she turned fifteen years old.

"My mother would give me these silly dresses to wear to school, not jeans. No jewelry. No makeup. And they'd always say, 'Stick with the Mexican kids. Don't talk to the Anglos. They'll boss you.'"

Her parents told her she could not date boys until after her fifteenth birthday and that the occasion would be celebrated with a *quinceanera*, the traditional coming-out party for girls. On that day, she was told, she would wear a frilly dress ordered by catalog from Mexico and dance her first dance with her father.

The party came and went just as her parents had planned it, but the next day she announced to them that she was pregnant and that she was moving out to live with her boyfriend. That night the boyfriend's mother, a third-generation Mexican American on welfare, served the couple plain boiled white rice.

"I had never eaten rice like that because my mother made it Mexican style," Imelda said. "When I ate that white rice at his house that night, I felt like an American. I was free."

In the course of just a few years, Imelda's identity had changed drastically, and it was certain to change still more before she reached adulthood. But what sort of identity will this change produce? And what models are available to help explain how young immigrants are developing their identities in U.S. cities? Since the children of Latino immigrants are expected to be the fastest-growing category of the U.S. population for the rest of this decade, the answers to these questions will be vitally important for years to come.

Young people like Imelda are a surging cultural force that has the potential to overthrow traditional ideas about how people become Americans and how ethnic groups function in U.S. society.

The melting pot is the oldest and most familiar model used to describe what happens to immigrants once in the United States. It is most potently symbolized by those who changed their names at Ellis Island so that they would fit better into the new society. There is something very American about Imelda's fate as a teenage single mother, but she was not simply shedding her Mexican identity to conform with American ways.

The idea that immigrant identity simply dissolves into an American "oneness" was authoritatively declared dead almost thirty years ago by Nathan Glazer and Daniel P. Moynihan in their book, *Beyond the Melting Pot*. The "point about the melting pot," they wrote, "is that it did not happen." They went on to argue that "this is nothing remarkable. On the contrary, the American ethos is nowhere better perceived than in the disinclination of the third and fourth generation of newcomers to blend into a standard uniform national type."[1]

A more contemporary alternative is the multicultural model. David Dinkins, the former mayor of New York, seemed to capture the concept when he described his city as a "gorgeous mosaic." In this idealized metropolis, many ethnic and racial groups live in equality alongside each other, but each group remains essentially apart. Proponents of the multiculturalism argue that there is no common American identity, or at least none worth assimilating into, and so immigrants should retain their distinct ethnic personalities.

Yet Imelda does not seem to be someone who is asserting a cultural identity deeply imbedded in her ethnicity any more than she seems to be blending into a standard national type.

These two models of ethnic identity in the United States are now the subject of bitter ideological dispute. But the new immigrants have virtually no role in this conflict except as fodder for the debate. The most devoted combatants are academics and pundits, and the major battlegrounds are university curricula and rules of free speech. While immigrants may have very little interest in the vicissitudes of political correctness, they are deeply affected by this rift in the American intellectual landscape.

Neither side of this debate, however, offers much of a model for the way ethnicity is playing itself out in American cities today. Nonetheless, perceptions and policies that affect the everyday life of immigrants are being shaped by the conflict. As the two sides become further polarized and hardened in their positions, they move farther and farther from reality as lived in places like East Los Angeles, or Houston's old ship channel wards, or Hialeah, Florida.

THE NEW ETHNICITY: DYNAMIC AND ENDURING

The life and times of these places demand a new model for ethnic identity in immigrant communities. Just as the melting pot model projects a sense of ethnicity that is too unanchored, the mosaic is too static. Immigrants do not blend into a uniform national type, but neither do they retain fixed and distinct ethnic identities forever. Accurately depicting life in Latino immigrant community requires a vision of ethnic identity as something both dynamic and enduring; fluid, ambiguous, and adaptive, but still distinctive.

First, it is important to set aside European notions of ethnic identity. To describe someone as Polish, Irish, German, or Italian conveys a commonly understood set of assumptions about language, history, high culture, politics, social behavior, cuisine, and even appearance. The European wave of migration to the United States began as the rise of nationalism sharpened these identities. The wave crested as violent assertions of national identity produced a long period of bloodletting that culminated in the Third Reich. Latin America has yet to produce any ethnic identity as rigid or as militant as that.

Given the historical context, it is hardly surprising that each group of European immigrants brought a distinct ethnic identity to the United States. For the full hundred-year history of the migration, each ethnic group made aggressive use of that identity to establish its place here, whether that meant Irish domination of the Roman Catholic Church, establishment of German-language schools, or publishing of native-language newspapers. Several factors produce a more ambiguous and adaptive form of ethnicity among Latinos.

Virtually every nation in Latin America is racially heterogeneous. Not only do the populations include people of several races, but also most of the people are of mixed blood. Moreover, national differences are mitigated by the sharing of both language and culture. And despite a variety of international wars and conflicts in the region, these are nations with relatively short histories.

Today's immigrants bring with them their own national identities, of course, but those identities are not as cohesive or comprehensive as those of the earlier Europeans. Complicating matters further is the notion of a pan-Latin ethnic identity. While clear national differences do exist all across Latin America, there is a sense of commonality and kinship that encompasses the various nations of the hemisphere. That does not translate, however, into any overarching identity as "Latinos" or "Hispanics."

Most of the people who might actually call themselves either "Hispanic" or "Latino" reject both terms. For example, the Latino National Political Survey, one of the most extensive efforts ever undertaken to measure attitudes among Latinos, found little interest in labels that lumped everyone with Latin American roots into one group. Instead, the respondents clearly preferred to identify themselves as "Mexican Americans," "Puerto Ricans," or other such terms based on national origins.[2]

All of this suggests that the concept of an ethnic group is applied to Latinos simply because no other paradigm readily exists. And if the formula for grouping people ethnically breaks down with such a large part of the population, then one can assume that the growth of the Hispanic population may lead to a fundamental redefinition of ethnicity and its workings.

After all, immigration and its influence over the urban experience have always been the engine of ethnicity in American society. Today, it is driving the concept in new directions.

U.S. cities are even more heterogeneous places in the 1990s than they were when a dozen distinct European nationalities inhabited them. The population of almost every major metropolitan area can be broken into four major racial groups—blacks, whites, Asians, and Latinos—with dozens of ethnic and national subgroups among them.

It is wrong to assume that everyone who comes to the United States from the same place will march forward together toward the same identity. Every individual immigrant's experience increases the diversity of Latino ethnic forms in the United States.

Geographic dispersal and widely differing rates of upward mobility create enormous differences among people who came from the same country, even from the same village. While some live in an ethnic enclave barely speaking English, others scatter through the suburban landscape and constantly renegotiate their identities with the Anglo mainstream.

Both the melting pot model and the mosaic model also fail to take into account the exceptional degree of interaction among individuals of different ethnic origins now taking place in U.S. cities, producing all sorts of intermarriage and hybridization far from the mainstream. One of the more dramatic examples of this is the absorption of black urban culture by Latino immigrants. Spanish rap music and baggy shorts on members of Chicano gangs are a form of assimilation, though by no means an adoption of a single "national identity."

Finally, any conception of ethnicity in today's immigrant communities must take into account the vast array of influences that now shape ethnic identities. Young people are bombarded by a consumer culture that becomes their main source of ideas about the United States. Yet even as they adapt to this America they see around them, new immigrants constantly arrive to remind them of their ethnic roots. On the one hand, young people like Imelda are throttled forward toward mainstream American society; on the other, they are constantly pulled back to the culture and language of their parents' homelands.

Rather than simply assimilating, as believers in the melting pot theory would prefer, or holding on to their native ways as the multiculturalists would suggest, Latino immigrants are developing new ethnic identities through their experience in the United States. Whether it is the *chicanos* of Los Angeles, the Mexican Americans of south Texas, the *Nuyoricans* of East Harlem, or the Cubans from Miami, there is no doubt that the current wave is producing many distinct and novel forms of ethnic expression.

ETHNICITY AND ECONOMIC STATUS

Latino ethnicity in the United States is ambiguous, dynamic, and diverse, but there is another side to it as well. Within a single Latino group there are sharp differences in ethnic character that depend on an individual's economic status. Frank D. Bean and Marta Tienda, in their landmark 1987 study for the Russell Sage Foundation, *The Hispanic Population of the United States*, explored the diversity of the Latino personalities in the United States and concluded that Hispanic ethnicity is heavily conditioned by this nation's "stratified society" in which skin color and economic status jointly determine a person's place. Bean and Tienda note that among successful Hispanics ethnicity often acquires a symbolic quality that is primarily manifested by continued observance of holidays, the consumption of ethnic foods, and other such ritual traits, "while in the areas of occupation, education, language, and residence they have increasingly modeled Anglos."

The character of those who do not make it economically is very different. Bean and Tienda describe a nexus of immigrant ethnicity, discrimination, and civil rights politics. That intersection is the key to understanding the most visible, but not necessarily the most numerous, Latinos—the urban poor. For Hispanics relegated to poverty and to life in urban *barrios*, Bean and Tienda found that "ethnicity becomes synonymous with minority status." As such, ethnicity is more than an expression of cultural heritage or a reflection of an economic condition. Among poor, segregated Latinos, ethnic identity is a powerful defense mechanism that, according to Bean and Tienda, "offers refuge to its adherents against the very system that produces stratification and oppression."

The fact that Latinos develop different identities at different strata of American society indicates that class differences have more than just an economic impact on new immigrants. These divisions not only determine how individuals adapt to the United States, but they also decisively limit the Latino population's ability to form a coherent interest group capable of achieving political influence.

In their 1992 report, "Latino Voices," the team of scholars that conducted the Latino National Political Survey concluded, "over all, these groups do not constitute a political community." Latinos from all over the country, time and again, did not rise to the bait when the survey posed questions that could have provoked displays of ethnic bias. A clear majority of citizens and noncitizens alike agreed there was too much immigration and that people from Latin America should not receive preference in immigration policy. Moreover, Latinos overwhelmingly agreed with the proposition that people living in the United States should learn to speak English. The noncitizens displayed an almost gushing enthusiasm for American ideals. They were twice as likely as non-Hispanic whites to agree with the proposition that "government is run for the benefit of all."

Referring to the majority of the survey's respondents, the scholars reported, "Their positive views on their experiences with government and their optimism about their future suggest that the relationship between these groups is not so harsh as to isolate the 'Hispanic' community and make it easily mobilized around narrow ethnic appeals." As with all conclusions drawn from surveys, these findings depict the behavior of an aggregate. The survey merely illustrates the fact that the whole Hispanic population does not respond as one entity and that overall it does not display ethnic alienation. Individual communities, however, are perfectly capable of behaving as coherent groups and pursuing what appear to be ethnic interests, even narrow ones.

During the last great wave of immigration, ethnic solidarity played a major role in helping newcomers adjust to the United States and easing them through their financial and social problems. In their jockeying for political position, well-established communities of Italians, Poles, Irish, and others worked hard to make citizens out of newly arrived immigrants, because ethnic-bloc voting led to power and patronage.

Given the unique character of the Hispanic population, as well as changes in the nation's economy and political system, it is unlikely those patterns will repeat themselves precisely. Government today plays a much larger role in ensuring social welfare, and at the same time there is far less public engagement in electoral politics. The new immigrants are coming to cities without effective institutions. What happens to them politically will be a matter of inventing something new and not adapting the patterns of the past.

If Latinos in fact do not emerge as a cohesive political community, the implications will resound to the very foundations of contemporary political life. Regardless of the outcome, the current wave of migration will mark a new chapter in the history of ethnic relations in the United States.

THE NEW ETHNICITY AND THE CIVIL RIGHTS STRUGGLE

Since the 1960s, the civil rights concept has governed ethnic relations in the United States. This concept is based on the stark, clear divisions between whites and blacks. It requires individuals to identify themselves as members of a group and to pursue their interests as members of a single political community. The legacy of white and black race relations also separates all groups into either "minority" or "majority," and those that have a recognized grievance against society and those who don't.

The dynamism and diversity of Hispanic identities suggest that this rapidly growing population will not fit the civil rights paradigm for much longer. The need for group solidarity and broad agreement on a single agenda seems to run counter to the rapid pace of change, diversity, and polarization so evident within the nation's Latino population. But if Latinos do not function as a political community under current definitions, this does not mean they will simply disappear into the Anglo mainstream without a trace.

There are long-standing grievances among native-born Latinos that will become the basis for political action. There may not be a single national agenda, but there are many local agendas that will be fought for, such as the legacies of segregation in the Texas schools, the use of the apportionment process to limit Hispanic political representation in California, the ongoing abuse of farm workers in the Southwest, and decades of neglect and poor administration in the New York City schools.

Moreover, language does appear to be an issue that can inspire group solidarity. The experience of "English-only" and "English-first" initiatives shows that Latinos are ready, willing, and able to speak English but prefer to do it without intimidation. The Cuban community of Miami, for example, has learned enough English to help build that city into a thriving center of international banking and commerce and to play an influential role in U.S. politics. Nonetheless, in 1993 these groups came together forcefully to repeal a thirteen-year-old Dade County ordinance mandating the use of English in official business. It is worth noting that while they came together successfully on this language issue, a few months later they were too divided to elect one of the members of their own community as city mayor.

In sum, it is clear that the current wave of immigration is changing the dynamics of ethnicity in the United States. But the transformation is still very much in progress. It is also certain that Latinos represent a potent ethnic force, but that their ethnicity expresses itself in many distinct forms and in pursuit of many different goals.

For the moment it is best to pose questions: Will some form of pan-ethnic Latino identity develop in the United States, and what shape might it take if it does? Or will many different Hispanic identities develop based on class, region, and nationality? Will some coalition of interests develop between African Americans and Hispanics? Or will they cease to identify with each other under the minority-group umbrella? What are the chances that Latino immigration will produce an entirely new concept of political community? Is there a model that relies less on grievance than the civil rights paradigm? Is there a way around the European concept of ethnic identity as something that separates and excludes? If there are answers to any of these questions, they may well emerge out of barrios of the United States.

The one certainty is that the old models no longer suffice. Latino immigrants are not obliged to choose between becoming ethnic plaintiffs or surrendering their identity. That is a false choice because it fails to appreciate the extent to which Latino immigration has already transformed the ethnic landscape of the United States, a transformation most apparent in its great cities.

CHAPTER 10

IMMIGRATION TO THE BURN ZONE

During Los Angeles' days of fury in spring 1992, the sounds of gunfire and helicopters reminded Elsa Flores why she had left El Salvador and made her wonder what she had accomplished by coming to the United States.

As the rioting flared all around her home in the South Central part of the city, Mrs. Flores bundled her family into a back room of their little bungalow and from this refuge they watched the mayhem on television. On the second day of the disturbances, an image televised from a helicopter showed a landscape that seemed especially familiar, and Mrs. Flores realized that the building in which her small clothing business was housed was on fire. Once an abandoned warehouse, the building had been converted into a big indoor flea market when the neighborhood had become solidly Latino during the immigrant influx of the 1980s. Many Salvadoran newcomers like Mrs. Flores rented space there and sold their goods off folding tables. Other immigrants came to buy goods at cheap prices. Now the whole place was in flames.

"I watched and held my daughters," said Mrs. Flores, who had worked nine years as a salesclerk to save the money to set up her own stall. "As it burned I held them tighter and tighter, and as I watched the flames I thought, 'It is all lost, all lost, everything I've earned in this country, all lost.'"

More than a year and a load of debt later, Mrs. Flores opened another clothing stand at another swap meet. But she measures her losses in more than money. The lessons she and other Latino immigrants draw from the riots will reshape the city. Do they stay and continue to invest? Do they leave and join the swelling Latino exodus to the suburbs? Do they simply surrender to the forces that have made the community around them a war zone and watch as

71

their children assimilate to the culture of self-destruction so evident in the fires that burned that spring?

"In this kind of neighborhood you have to learn to live with worry about all the crime and the drugs and the gangs, and I thought I had," Mrs. Flores said. "After this I don't know. In El Salvador there is violence, but you can understand it. But here I ask myself, how can it be that in such a big and developed nation there can be so much violence?"

For her and thousands of other Latino immigrants, the appeal of South Central, an overwhelmingly black neighborhood just a few years ago, was the presence of cheaper and less crowded housing than in the city's older barrios. Now she and her husband, who has his own flea market stall, are wondering whether the inner city is such a good place to raise daughters ten and three years old.

A small woman with broad shoulders who bargains hard with every customer, Mrs. Flores said, "I know people who have moved out to parts of the city far away, even the desert. They say it is better for hard-working people. I've thought about it, but it is hard to think that all we are doing is so we can pick up and start over."

NEW WARNINGS FROM CHANGING CITIES

The Los Angeles riot is often compared to the black ghetto uprisings of the 1960s. They are similar in that they all served as warnings, but the 1992 riot warned of new problems in a new type of city marked by massive immigration.

Every year hundreds of thousands of new Latino immigrants pour into the nation's cities as urban whites and blacks move out in ever-increasing numbers. These newcomers are by far the largest single group of new entrants to the urban population, and they are learning to become Americans amid myriad urban ills. Each of them is attempting to absorb this new culture; either adapting to it or in some cases becoming alienated from it. Altogether they are transforming the cities even as the cities are transforming them.

While the anger of blacks toward Korean store owners grabbed headlines during the riot, it is now apparent that Latinos played a much larger role than was commonly acknowledged. Some 51 percent of the people arrested were Latinos, as were some 30 percent of the dead. And Latinos owned nearly 40 percent of the damaged businesses, according to a study by the Tomás Rivera Center, a Latino think-tank based in Claremont, California.[1] Both perpetrators and victims, the Latinos of Los Angeles suffered the ultimate indignity when the disturbance was depicted solely as a race riot.

Los Angeles is not the only place in which Latino immigrants have expressed their alienation through violence in the streets. It happened in New York's predominately Dominican Washington Heights neighborhood in July

1992, and in Washington's heavily Salvadoran Mount Pleasant community in May 1991.

During the 1980s the immigrant influx brought about a rejuvenation of many urban neighborhoods with a blossoming of small businesses, especially in the retail and construction sectors. Inner cities today are full of people like Mrs. Flores, who struggle to make a life for themselves with few assets other than their grit and determination. With a firm foothold in the middle class, some newcomers move out of immigrant enclaves to safer neighborhoods elsewhere. Others are working just as hard but remain locked in lives of poverty, fearing for children who too often succumb to the culture of the city streets.

What will be the ratio of immigrant success stories compared to the tales of urban woe? The answer to that question, more than anything else, will determine how this era of migration changes the United States. Indeed, no set of quotas, no border enforcement strategies, no aspect of immigration policy makes any sense unless this question is answered first.

RELATIVE SUCCESS STORIES

The 1990 census showed that about a third of all recent Latino immigrants are concentrated at the low end of the labor force, where full-time work produces little more than a life of poverty. But despite disadvantages of language and culture, adult immigrants often cope with poverty better than the native born. Economic difficulties are frequently mitigated by the powerful workings of family networks that are as active here as they are in sending communities. By sharing resources, they are able to make more of their small income than Americans leading more fragmented lives, and by sharing job information they can often ensure steady work for their kin.

This life of working poverty represents a measure of upward mobility for many immigrants from Latin America. Seeing their rewards in the remittances they send home, and often convinced they themselves will return home to enjoy those gains, they see success in an economic status that most native-born Americans would consider indigent.

By several measures, the poverty-level work force of Latino immigrants may be considered an asset for the United States. These workers fill an obvious demand in the labor market, and they bring a healthy influx of incomes to inner-city communities.

MEASURING SUCCESS IN THE SECOND GENERATION

The real challenge lies not with the immigrants but with their children. Newcomers are expected to endure economic and social difficulties in any society. This has always been the immigrant's lot, but the immigrant's offspring are expected to do better. The success of any wave of immigration is ultimately measured by the achievements of the second and the third generations. Consequently, as the nation debates what levels of immigration it can absorb, it must determine how much it can offer the children of immigrants and whether it permits enough of them to realize the American dream of leading better lives than their parents.

In measuring the opportunities for upward mobility offered to children of Latino immigrants, it is instructive to look back at the European wave, especially the peak decades around the turn of the century. Although it is often forgotten in the rosy memories of Ellis Island immigration, the European wave also produced a large proportion of people who never made it out of the tenements. Indeed, in the later decades of the nineteenth century, life expectancy was greater for Irish males who stayed home than it was for those who went to the United States, where so many were felled by dangerous work, alcoholism, and the diseases that accompany poverty.[2] If one considers the condition of the immigrant poor from the 1880s until World War II ended the Great Depression, it is hard to imagine that the nation would countenance such misery today. But places like Hell's Kitchen and Chicago's river wards eventually became enclaves where European immigrants and their offspring could gather political strength. They fostered institutions like the Roman Catholic Church in American, labor unions, and political machines that helped them move into the American mainstream.

Urban enclaves were also a place to develop economic strength. European immigrants flowed almost exclusively into U.S. cities, and during the periods of peak influx those cities were great engines of economic growth as this country built its industrial economy. Latino immigrants are also concentrated in big cities, but the cities are a very different place now.

The unions and political machines are withered vestiges and the Catholic Church followed the European ethnics to the suburbs. Instead, there are epidemics of homelessness, crack, AIDS, gangs, and crime. Many city governments are broke, and Latinos often find themselves battling blacks for a share of the dwindling resources. Meanwhile, the engines of economic growth have moved away from the urban core to the suburbs and ex-urbs. All of this makes life harder for all city dwellers, but new arrivals face special challenges. Even as they must overcome the obstacles that defeated many of the native born, who are now relegated to the urban underclass, they must do so while learning a new language and new culture. The costs of remaining poor in the cities have gone up, and families with children have very little time before they begin to pay the price.

"I call it the 'East L.A. short circuit,'" said Art Revueltas. "The way it goes is that if you come from Mexico to East L.A. and you have kids, the clock is ticking on how long you've got to make it out. If you get stuck, the kids don't make it through school. So they don't make it out. Then you get teenage parents, and those kids won't make it out. All of a sudden you're talking about third-generation gang members."

Revueltas is the son of a Mexican immigrant who came to East Los Angeles, the city's oldest and biggest barrio. About a quarter of the Latino families there live in poverty, and some members of the street gangs do indeed trace their lineage back more than three generations. Revueltas and his family got out. He is now the vice principal of an intermediate school in Montebello, a Latino middle-class suburb of Los Angeles. A community of pastel-colored bungalows with neat lawns, it is just the sort of place that many Latinos, native born and immigrant alike, head for as soon as they have the money to leave the inner city. He is deeply worried that an ever-greater number of immigrants are getting short-circuited.

Looking back, the forty-year-old Revueltas sees that the immigrants of his parents' generation established themselves in the 1960s, when the industrial economy was still strong and government mortgage programs helped assure a supply of affordable quality housing. As a result, he went to college, and his parents helped him buy a home after he graduated. "They developed enough equity to allow me to become vested in the system," he said.

According to the classic formula used to describe the path taken by the immigrants of the European wave, it took three generations to climb the ladder. The immigrant generation worked the poverty-wage, entry-level jobs and lived in an ethnic neighborhood. The second generation was solidly Americanized and moved up into the working class with well-paid blue-collar jobs. If they didn't make it to the suburbs, their children did because the third generation went to college, became affluent, and rediscovered their ethnicity as "hyphenated" Americans. During the 1960s many Mexican Americans who had moved from the rural Southwest to the cities, and even many recently arrived immigrants, did well enough that they collapsed this progress into two generations, as with the Revueltas family.

THE BROKEN LADDER

What has changed? First, the costs of staying poor are much higher now than before. Homicide and incarceration rates among poor young males are a gruesome but accurate price index. Second, for people who immigrate into poverty (even more so for people born into poverty), the opportunities for upward mobility are more limited than in the past.

The later immigrants of the European wave and the first of their children had to endure the Great Depression. Indeed, the 1930s saw a net outmigration as many newcomers gave up and went home. In addition, birthrates dropped. Then World War II rejuvenated the industrial economy and served as a great crucible for a new American nationalism based on the promise of opportunity. After the war a rising economy and government programs like the GI Bill provided ladders of upward mobility. Now, those ladders have disappeared. Latino immigrants are creating a massive new generation during what has become a prolonged period of stagnant or declining incomes for most workers and of rising poverty even among the fully employed.

The current wave of migration began after the U.S. economy had begun shifting into the postindustrial era. One result of this restructuring has been a growing gap between high-income and low-income wage earners and an even greater distance between white and Latino workers. Contemporary institutions, most notably the public schools, do not provide bridges across that gap. Those at the entry level get stuck at the bottom and no longer make enough money to generate much momentum for their families. The blue-collar industrial jobs that required only modest skills but provided a decent income are increasingly scarce in the U.S. economy.

Wages for white males rose almost 27 percent in the 1960s in real terms, held steady in the 1970s, and then fell nearly 7 percent in the 1980s. The same inflation-adjusted wages for Latino males peaked in the 1960s, fell by more than 4 percent in the 1970s, and then collapsed with a loss of more than 11 percent in the 1980s. This happened during a time when Latinos were tripling their share of the work force.[3]

IMMIGRATION AND ECONOMIC RESTRUCTURING

Two major developments that began in the 1960s had substantially changed the shape of the labor force by the time the current wave of immigration reached big numbers in the 1980s.

The first was the rapid expansion of the service sector. The growth in finance, insurance, and business services is most often associated with a bounty of well-paid jobs and unprecedented opportunities for Anglo women. But as Sassen has documented in extensive studies of the New York City economy, "The expansion of the high-income work force in conjunction with the emergence of new cultural forms has led to a high-income gentrification that rests, in the last analysis, on the availability of a vast supply of low-wage workers."[4]

Sassen was describing the labor-intensive lifestyle of the "yuppy" during the 1980s. This was perhaps best symbolized by the gentrification of the Columbus and Amsterdam Avenue corridors on Manhattan's Upper West Side. As the apartment buildings became co-ops and the brownstones were renovated, the old ethnic establishments were replaced by upscale boutiques, specialty shops, restaurant, and bars. What were once working-class immigrant communities became glitzy neighborhoods where immigrants worked for minimum wage at dead-end jobs serving and cleaning up after a new population of affluent residents.

Although Sassen focuses on this as an urban phenomenon associated with the growth of the finance and the business sectors, Roger Rouse of the University of Michigan documented a similar situation in Redwood City, a bedroom community in northern California's Silicon Valley. The most recent migrants in a long-term flow from a small town in the Mexican state of Michoacán worked as the community's "janitors, dishwashers, gardeners, hotel workers, and house cleaners—proletarian servants in the paragon of 'post-industrial' societies."[5]

The second development that increased demand for low-wage immigrant workers occurred in the restructuring of manufacturing. The commonplace notion is that for at least twenty years or so the old Rust Belt manufacturing jobs have been either moving overseas or disappearing. In fact, even as many forms of manufacturing employment shrank, others grew. But this growth occurred either at the high end of the wage scale, in areas like aerospace or defense-related electronics, or at the low end, in areas like garments, food processing, and furniture production. Again, it was the migrants who poured into the low paid, low-wage jobs.

During the Los Angeles boom in the 1980s, female immigrants constituted 59 percent of the new entrants to the work force in nondurable-goods manufacturing, and immigrant men formed a similar share of new workers in durable goods. Despite this substantial presence in the industrial work force, recent immigrants were so heavily concentrated at the bottom that on average they earned just a bit more than a third of what Anglos were paid. While only one Anglo worker in eight labored at a minimum-wage job, about half of all recent Mexican migrants took home the lowest legal salary.[6]

At $4.25 an hour, the minimum wage that has prevailed since 1991, it currently takes nearly thirty-five hundred hours of work a year for a family of four to live above the federal poverty line. If one parent works a full forty hours a week and the other works twenty hours a week, they still won't cut it by the minimum standards set in Washington.

THE WORKING POOR

The new immigrants are poor, but they do not fit the image of urban poverty that has become commonplace in the United States since the 1960s. They suffer not from unemployment or underemployment, but from overemployment at poverty wages. The Tomás Rivera Center study of the Los Angeles riot, for example, found that in South Central more than 80 percent of the Hispanic males are in the labor force, compared to less than 60 percent of the community's non-Latino population, which is virtually all black. Even so, the Latinos of South Central are considerably poorer by several measures than their neighbors. Nearly 40 percent of the Latino families live below the poverty level, compared to about a quarter of the non-Latinos. The Latinos work many more hours than their black neighbors, but because they earn so little the Latinos still experience much greater poverty.[7]

Census data show that more than any other segment of society, Latino migrants, especially the recent arrivals, are the working poor (see Figure 10.1). The data also show that the way they survive is by sticking together (see Figures 10.2 and 10.3). When their income is measured on a per capita basis, about 30 percent of all Mexican immigrants fall below the poverty level, a rate almost as high as that for the African American population nationwide. But when their income is measured by household a very different picture emerges. While nearly 30 percent of all black households earn less than $10,000 a year, only about 20 percent of Mexican immigrant households endure that level of poverty. Remarkably, among the most recently arrived Salvadoran families, those who came in the 1980s, only 15 percent earn less than $10,000 a year, about the same as for the U.S. population as a whole.

Instead of being flat-out poor, immigrants are concentrated just one step ahead of poverty. Recent migrants especially are more likely than any other population group to be found in the annual income range of between $15,000 and $25,000 per household. Less than 18 percent of all families in the United

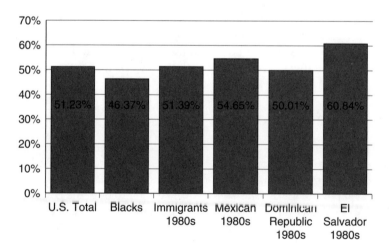

FIGURE 10.1
HOUSEHOLD INCOME
$15,000–$50,000

Source: U.S. Department of Commerce, Bureau of the Census, *1990 Census of Population.*

FIGURE 10.2
WORKERS PER FAMILY
Three or More

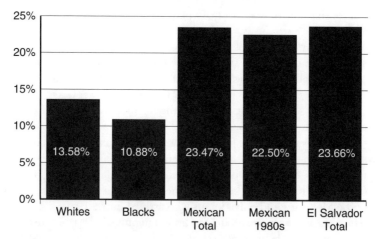

Source: U.S. Department of Commerce, Bureau of the Census, *1990 Census of Population.*

FIGURE 10.3
WORKERS PER FAMILY
Two or More

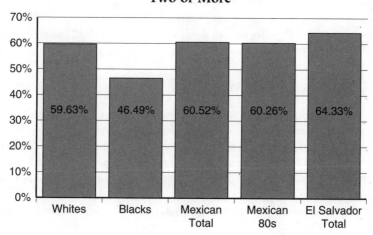

Source: U.S. Department of Commerce, Bureau of the Census, *1990 Census of Population.*

States are in that range, while about 27 percent of the most recently arrived Salvadorans and Mexicans earn that much. If one looks more broadly at working-class incomes, the range of $15,000 to $50,000 annually per household, 55 percent of the Mexicans and 61 percent of the Salvadorans who came in the 1980s make that much, while only 46 percent of black households are in the same category.

When many members of a population group, like recent Latino immigrants, lack education, work skills, or even a mastery of English, and many cannot work legally, it is logical to expect they will work for low wages. But then why do they do so well as households? Part of the answer lies in the strong family structures so important in getting the migrants here in the first place. Census figures show that among the Mexican and Salvadoran migrants of the 1980s, about 24 percent of the families draw incomes from three or more workers, while the same is true of only 11 percent of black families and 14 percent of Anglo families. Similarly, while 14 percent of Anglo families and 19 percent of black families have no workers at all, the same is true for only about 5 percent of the Mexicans and Salvadorans who arrived in the 1980s.[8]

These statistics are the product of an immigrant social structure that has become increasingly distinctive in the United States' inner cities. Its characteristics are intact families, a dogged work ethic, and kinship networks that provide vital cooperation and mutual assistance. An extensive survey conducted in Chicago poverty areas found that Mexican immigrants were more than twice as likely than blacks to be living as married couples with children. And Mexican immigrant women were five times less likely than blacks to be single mothers with children.[9] The study also found that Mexican immigrants show a stronger preference for work over welfare compared to blacks, and that the Latinos expressed attitudes toward welfare recipients markedly more negative than those held by blacks.

THE POWER OF NETWORKING

Even more important in economic terms than these attitudes, the Chicago study found that the immigrants share distinct advantages over blacks. Very often the immigrants benefit from tightly knit networks of friends and relatives who share information about jobs, care for one another's children, and otherwise help one another survive in an American urban culture not only alien to them but often dangerous.

These networks amount to a powerful "Latino civil society" in many urban areas, says Professor David Hayes-Bautista, a UCLA sociologist who is studying the immigrant social structure in South Central Los Angeles. "They come from cultures where people have survived poverty for centuries with little recourse to government or other institutions," he said. "Here they have very little connection to community groups or city agencies but they have established very effective linkages among themselves."

After Elsa Flores lost her clothing stall during the Los Angeles riots, for instance, she didn't even think about going to a bank or seeking reconstruction relief. "Those places always ask for a million papers and things that are impossible," she said. Instead, she rounded up $6,000 from friends and relatives to get started again. "They know I learned how to do this from my parents," she said.

The workings of kinship networks are no less important to understanding what happens to Latino immigrants once they settle in the United States than they are to understanding how the immigrants get here in the first place. It is the strength of household relationships, for example, that helps explain the phenomenal growth of Latino-owned businesses in the absence of any ready access to commercial credit.

A survey of minority-owned business in Los Angeles County showed that between 1972 and 1992 Latino-owned firms grew at a rate three times faster than the Latino population. Given how quickly the Latino population was growing, this meant that the number of those businesses multiplied sevenfold in those two decades. These businesses are not indicators of wealth, however.

Most of these businesses are small family-run operations that often take advantage of the informal labor market that flourishes in the barrios. More than 80 percent of Latino-owned firms in Los Angeles county were registered as having no paid staff, which leads to the assumption that the workers are primarily family members paid off the books. But even if these businesses are not great money-makers, they are a vivid display of entrepreneurship and self-reliance. Many of these firms are the small commercial establishments—the shops, restaurants, auto garages, and travel agencies—that have economically revitalized many neighborhoods, from the San Fernando Valley to Queens.[10]

For now, Mrs. Flores remains committed to living and doing business in the heart of Los Angeles. She and millions like her have managed to pull themselves up a few rungs of the ladder, but only that far. If they fall off, if the economy or the government pushes them off, they do not have far to fall before they hit bottom. And in United States cities today, very few people that hit bottom ever fully recover. As encouraging as the statistics on household income may seem, many of these immigrant families live but one step from a precipice.

In recent years a lively academic debate has developed over how to define the new immigrants' place in the U.S. labor force. George J. Borjas focuses on the education, skills, and other forms of human capital that the immigrants bring with them. Sassen describes the emergence of "global cities" in which the immigrant work force is one element of a vast international economy. Gregory DeFreitas has detailed the effects of discrimination, the decline of the labor movement, and other structural factors.

Coming at the issue from entirely different perspectives and often reaching widely disparate conclusions, all of these scholars point to the persistence of a large immigrant work force that is mired at the low end of the economy, and their explanations for the causes are not mutually exclusive. The immigrants' lack of marketable skills, the demands of globalized corporate structures, and the absence of structures to promote upward mobility are all contributing forces.

THE RISE OF THE SECOND GENERATION

Even for the one-third of Latino immigrants locked into lives of working poverty, the experience of coming to the United States is often a net plus both for them and for the country. But perhaps more important than the relative poverty of these people is whether their lives allow them to be good parents. The great mystery of this present wave of immigration is the fate of the second generation, the children of the immigrants of the 1980s and 1990s. This question is critical because of the size of this generation. Half of the Hispanic population, some eleven million people, were less than twenty-five years old in 1990, while only a third of the Anglo population were in that age category.

According to Census Bureau estimates, the size of the Hispanic population will double between 1990 and 2015, triple by 2035, and quadruple by 2050. And these projections are based on the assumption that "this growth of the Hispanic population over the next six decades may be influenced more by natural increase than immigration." As a demographic event, this growth in the Hispanic population will be as significant as the baby boom. Its significance arises not just from its size, but also because of its rate of growth in comparison with other groups.

The growth of the non-Hispanic white population has already stalled, and it will actually begin declining in size after the year 2035, according to current projections. The black population, meanwhile, will grow modestly. The Asian population will grow quickly, but from a very small base. Latinos, however, will contribute nearly half of the nation's population growth by the year 2020, which is only twenty-five years away.[11]

Clearly the United States has a real stake in the enormous generation of children of the current wave of immigrants. They are literally the future of the country. Given the pace of social, technological, and economic change, it seems a bogus exercise to predict their fate. As immigrants disembarked at Ellis Island in 1910, no one could have foreseen what the world would be like for their children in 1935 and grandchildren in 1960.

Such uncertainty is of course no excuse for inaction, especially given the worrisome symptoms already evident. Two interrelated problems cloud the future of the children of today's immigrants: lack of economic mobility and a failing educational system. Finding a solution to these problems is complicated by the fact that the Latino immigrant population does not fit neatly into the structures of ethnic group politics in the United States.

As a whole, Latino young people, and especially the children of recent immigrants, are the poorest sector of the population, and there are real questions about how much upward mobility they can expect. While the bottom rungs of the ladder are open to just about anyone who is willing and able-bodied, the jobs in the middle and higher rungs require ever-increasing qualifications. Education has become the primary source of upward mobility in the postindustrial economy, and there are many indications that Latino migrants are not doing well in school.

The American Council of Education calculates that nationwide the Hispanic dropout rate is nearly 50 percent, compared with 20 percent for the population as a whole. A massive survey of the children of immigrants, being conducted by Alejandro Portes and various collaborators, found that the children of Mexican immigrants lagged far behind the mean in several measures of educational achievement. More worrisome still, the survey found that the longer young people live here, the more likely they are to adopt bad habits, such as studying less and watching television more, so grades decline in proportion to the time they have been here.[12] And whatever happens to the U.S. economy, it seems certain that high school dropouts will be lucky to find themselves with minimum-wage jobs.

Instead of serving as models for the repair of the urban landscape, many immigrant families find themselves on a slippery slope. Their children have little prospect for economic advancement and are beset by all the urban epidemics. If the poverty rate is 30 percent among Mexican immigrants, is it possible that the dropout rates predict that it will be more than 50 percent among their children? What would be the social costs of that outcome? If today's Latino dropouts are no more than candidates for a life of frustration and poverty, then the fires of Los Angeles were a grim warning indeed. This specter of persistent poverty among Latino migrants can only be addressed by first examining illegal immigration and the resulting political volatility about the costs of education and social programs for the immigrants.

CHAPTER 11

ILLEGAL ALIENS, ILLEGAL JOBS

Throughout the current wave of immigration, one aspect of the event—illegal immigration—has commanded an overwhelming share of public attention. It has been posed as a law enforcement problem of porous borders, as a fiscal problem of unwanted migrants draining public resources, and occasionally as a political problem of a large population deprived of the full benefits of living in U.S. society.

At its core illegal immigration is an economic problem. If properly framed it does highlight one of the most difficult policy challenges arising from contemporary migration—that of deciding how much the government should try to influence the economic forces that ultimately determine the immigrants' place in U.S. society. Chief among these forces is the economy's appetite for low-wage labor. In fact, the demand for people to work for poverty-level pay has resulted in two of the most dangerous aspects of the current wave of migration:

The first is that the growth of the low-wage economy is accelerating the polarization of our society along a fault line of class and ethnicity. About a third of all Latino immigrants live a life of working poverty. Adults are fully employed, often with more than one job apiece, but they still do not earn enough money to provide their children with the bare necessities of a decent life. As noted previously, immigrants who work for poverty wages and their children are only one step from the oblivion of the underclass. Every increase in the population of working poor increases the pool of candidates for the poverty of dependence or the poverty of crime. Moreover, in the absence of effective urban schools and with a labor force that has ever fewer jobs in the middle range of skills and pay, there is little chance of upward mobility for the children of impoverished workers, leading to an ever-greater sense of alienation among the next generation.

The second result of soaring illegal immigration is the growth of the informal, or black market, economy. Anywhere from a fifth to a third of all migrants enter the country illegally and live an underground existence. This large population facilitates the growth of an underground economy in which employers ignore laws regarding wages, benefits, worker safety, and the payment of taxes.

The very presence of so many illegal aliens has helped turn the low-wage economy into a self-perpetuating monster, which is gradually becoming immune to corrective measures by government. The experience of several European governments has shown that each effort to improve the low-wage sector by raising wages or benefits has resulted in a larger number of jobs moving into the black economy, where they are filled by illegal immigrants. As a result, researchers in both Germany and Italy have recently concluded that in the absence of effective control over illegal immigration, efforts to improve conditions for low-wage workers often have the opposite effect. Instead of paying the extra costs when standards are raised, employers turn to illegal workers and the overall conditions of the jobs actually decline.

What does the European experience portend for the United States? If, for example, the Clinton administration fulfills its promises to increase the minimum wage and to enact a universal health insurance program, the one certain result will be an increase in labor costs. In the face of such increased costs, many marginally profitable businesses will simply turn to the employment of illegal aliens in jobs that are off the books and that pay substandard wages and no health benefits. The alternative, as described below, is to do both at once— raise the status of low-wage workers and reduce the influx of illegal migrants as part of a coordinated strategy.

Two other important factors arise from illegal immigration, both of which affect the treatment of legal immigrants and both of which need to be addressed by the American public. The first is that the existence of a large population of illegal aliens makes it virtually impossible to build political support for government programs to help ensure the successful integration of legal immigrants into both the culture and the economy. The second is the broader issue of social justice. Americans should be made to consider whether it is proper to maintain a work force of several million foreign laborers who are set apart from the mainstream of society by language and ethnicity and who work for wages that relegate them to poverty. More to the point, Americans should consciously decide whether they feel comfortable personally profiting from the labor of these workers, whether as employers or consumers.

AN ABORTED SOLUTION

These are not new issues. More than a decade of study and debate preceded the enactment of the Immigration Reform and Control Act of 1986. That process involved the efforts of the Ford, Carter, and Reagan administrations, a presidential commission, and three all-out debates in Congress. Along the way, the full array of interest groups had their say in developing the law. Labor unions, church groups, the manufacturing industry, farmers, civil rights organizations, immigration advocates as well as opponents, and many others were deeply involved.

What was most remarkable about this process was that it actually resulted in a near-unanimous consensus, with all of the parties essentially agreed on three points:

- Maintaining a large population of illegal aliens was bad for society and bad for the migrants.

- Work was the magnet that drew most of these people to the United States.

- Denying illegal migrants access to jobs was the best means to deter future illegal migrations.

Despite a great deal of controversy over specific measures, there was widespread agreement on the two-part strategy embodied in the 1986 law. On the one hand, it gave an amnesty to the existing population of illegal aliens. On the other, it attempted to cut the future flow with employer sanctions—a law enforcement effort that would take aim at employers, not migrants.

There were two major exceptions to this consensus. Latino advocacy groups argued that employer sanctions would increase job discrimination against all Latinos, but despite considerable evidence from government studies to support their claims, they failed to win any substantial concessions. The other main objection came from agricultural interests in California and the Southwest, which insisted that food prices would skyrocket and production would plummet unless they had access to cheap immigrant labor. Despite evidence that their claims of hardship were unjustified, the growers did win major concessions.

Even though the 1986 law represented an extraordinary level of agreement on a thorny set of issues, the agreed-upon strategy was never fully implemented. Some complex technical questions were never addressed, such as how to create documentation system that would allow employers to easily verify a job applicant's immigration status. And Washington never produced the money to pay for the personnel needed to enforce the law and simultaneously curtail its discriminatory effects.

These failings have been extensively studied and documented in congressional hearings, investigations by the General Accounting Office, and a lengthy research project conducted by the Rand Corporation and the Urban Institute.[1] Overall, this literature suggests that existing laws offer viable tools to seriously reduce the levels of illegal immigration. The problem is that, as with so much immigration policy, illegal immigration was viewed in the 1986 reform as a law enforcement problem, when in fact it is primarily an economic and social issue. Employer sanctions attacked the wrong end of the problem, trying to change the composition of the work force rather than the quality of the jobs.

The assumption underlying employer sanctions was that if the penalties for hiring illegal aliens were credibly enforced, employers would no longer hire them and the migrants would stay home. And by all accounts employer sanctions have succeeded in producing a deterrent effect among legitimate employers. In corporate personnel offices it is now a routine matter for new employees to fill out a form, the I-9, detailing their citizenship or immigration status and presenting documents that verify that status.

VIOLATING MANY LAWS WITH ONE JOB

The law, however, has failed to stem illegal immigration for a number of reasons. When employer sanctions were enacted, its supporters frequently drew a parallel to the payment of income taxes. The Internal Revenue Service knows that it has to conduct a certain number of audits and prosecutions each year so that the threat of punishment remains credible. Compared to the total number of taxpayers, the number of these actions is quite small, but they produce a deterrent effect that brings about a very high level of voluntary compliance.

There is a basic fallacy in trying to extend this enforcement strategy to the employment of illegal aliens. The people who voluntarily comply with the tax code, generally, are not in the process of committing other crimes in the way they make money or pay taxes. But, as was so aptly illustrated in the controversy surrounding Zoe Baird's nomination for attorney general, an employer who hires an illegal migrant is usually breaking a number of laws simultaneously. Employers of illegal aliens frequently fail to pay Social Security, withhold income taxes, maintain proper accounts, pay overtime, or otherwise respect laws regarding wages, benefits, and working conditions. Even if Zoe Baird's had hired U.S. citizens to help around her house and treated them the way she did her undocumented Peruvian servants, she would still have been violating several laws.

Indeed, the major reason why illegals are choice candidates for such work is that they are willing victims. Since their own illegality makes them unlikely to go to the authorities, they enable an employer to violate all sorts of other laws. Clearly, the financial benefit to an employer of illegal aliens does not result directly from their undocumented status, but from the ability to avoid compliance with many of the laws and regulations that raise the cost of labor.

In other words, it is a not just the type of employee that is in violation of the law but rather the entire circumstance of employment that is illegal. The policy focus must therefore change from illegal aliens to illegal jobs. Such a shift would be not just a matter of enforcement strategy, but would also imply a basic change in objective. The problem of illegal immigration is fundamentally intertwined with the existence of a large work force earning poverty wages, and the intersection of these concerns is in the illegal jobs.

When the 1986 reform was enacted, Congress, the Reagan administration, and a great many other players all decided that they wanted to eliminate, or at least greatly reduce illegal immigration. They did not, however, commit themselves to eliminating the jobs held by illegal aliens and others in the poverty-level work force.

This was most obvious in the agricultural sector, in which demands by the growers produced a special amnesty that had much laxer rules for farm workers than did the general amnesty. Because the authors of the 1986 act were unwilling to face the economic consequences of changing the structure of the labor force in such a way as to deter illegal immigration, more than a million people have already achieved resident status under this program. Although the workers were given an amnesty and the employment of illegal aliens was outlawed, the existence of the jobs remained untouched. As a result, amnesty recipients were able to move on to better employment. But their places were quickly taken by newly arrived undocumented workers, who are still earning poverty wages.

THE COSTS OF ENFORCEMENT

The alternative would be an aggressive effort to attack the entire range of unlawful behavior by employers of the poverty-level work force. In effect, law enforcement would take aim at the illegal jobs and not at the illegal workers. Making such a decision, however, would involve a variety of difficult considerations far beyond the usual parameters of immigration policy.

Take, for example, the women's sportswear industry in Los Angeles. During most of the recent recession it was the only sector of manufacturing that grew in southern California. It has attracted foreign capital, mostly from Asia, and it has actually drawn back to the United States some of the jobs that went overseas in search of cheaper labor. This return is a response to the fact that designers need to make quick and frequent changes in their production lines, and they need to assure a high level of quality control, something much easier to do in downtown Los Angeles than over the phone to Hermosillo or Manila. Ostensibly this is an economic success story. The work force of this garment industry, however, includes a high proportion of illegal aliens who labor in sweatshops, do piecework, and earn poverty wages. They have no health insurance, no benefits, and no dignity.

As a law enforcement matter, it would be a relatively simple matter to put together a federal task force of officials from the Immigration and Naturalization Service, the Internal Revenue Service, the Occupational Safety and Health Administration, the Environmental Protection Agency, the Department of Labor, and miscellaneous other agencies to sweep through the garment district and shut down or fine the employers found to be violating laws in order to keep labor costs down.

The garment industry, however, is highly competitive, both domestically and internationally. And it is very labor intensive. So any effort to raise wages and conditions to legal standards might simply oblige those factories to move overseas to a Third World country. But if these are Third World jobs, aren't we as a nation better off letting them go to the Third World? Is it really better to import workers and oblige them to live in Third World conditions right here in our cities, just so we can keep the jobs within our borders?

But what if the nation decides there is some essential strategic interest involved in keeping those jobs in the United States? Would it be worth paying more for the product to keep the jobs here? Or perhaps the nation is intent on eating its cake and having it too, that is, keeping the garment industry in the country and keeping prices for its products down. If so, Americans must be willing to tolerate the social costs of illegal immigration and a poverty-level work force.

Garments are just one example. Illegal workers are also employed in the production of custom auto parts, toys, furniture, and many other manufactured goods. Because of the sizable number of jobs at stake, the answers to these questions will have considerable economic consequences. A survey of applicants for the 1986 amnesty found that more than a quarter had been working in manufacturing. That is about 400,000 manufacturing jobs in California alone, more than the entire number of jobs lost in that state due to the downsizing of the defense industry.[2]

Aside from manufacturing, there is another large segment of jobs that currently pays poverty wages but that cannot leave the country. These are the janitors, dishwashers, babysitters, fruit pickers, painters, yardmen, construction laborers. In many cases these immigrants do work such as cleaning houses and caring for children, that was traditionally performed by working-class and middle-class women before those women joined the labor force. In others cases, these illegal workers simply lower the price of getting a car waxed or having a new roof put on a home. Since these jobs will not go overseas, they pose a rather simple question: How much are people willing to pay to have these tasks performed? The answer could have complex consequences.

The current prices reflect the wages paid to a largely immigrant work force that lives in poverty and that includes a very high percentage of illegal aliens. If this work force is considered a problem, either because of the long-term social effects of poverty labor or because illegal aliens are considered objectionable per se, then the solution will necessarily involve paying more for these services. This will be the result regardless of whether the goal is simply to reduce illegal immigration or to improve the conditions of low-wage workers in general. The essential policy decision will involve the government's willingness to affect the cost and availability of the services performed by this work force. Law enforcement strategies should be considered only after dealing with these economic considerations.

Are people concerned enough about the problems that arise from illegal immigration to pay an extra 30 or 40 or 50 percent for a cheap dinner out on a weeknight? Are they concerned enough to accept a rise in the consumer price index of 1 percent, along with a corresponding increase in interest rates? And are they concerned enough to accept the bankruptcy of a number of U.S.-based companies, because without a doubt many would fail if there were full and determined enforcement of rules on the employment of illegal aliens, payment of overtime, payment of Social Security taxes, and the full range of labor standards. Or is it more acceptable, politically and economically and morally, to enjoy the current wage structure for services and to accept the consequences of illegal immigration and a large, low-wage work force?

On top of all these questions, an important ideological issue must also be resolved. Action in any of these spheres would require new and aggressive forms of government intervention in the economy. A federal bureaucracy would have to decide where to attack and how hard to strike. And it means that work-place violations, including but not limited to the employment of illegal immigrants, would be given a major priority in law enforcement. Many Americans, even those who want to control illegal immigration, might object to the granting of such powers to a bureaucracy.

Finally, there is the simple issue of how much such a plan of action would cost. The public would have to accept new costs for federal manpower over a long period of time. Taking meaningful steps against illegal employment would involve deploying thousands, not dozens, of federal agents, magistrates, and prosecutors. And it would mean keeping up the pressure for years, not months.

An assessment of the efforts outlined above could readily be mistaken as an argument for inaction. It is not. There are real and substantial dangers in allowing a demographic force as powerful as illegal immigration to be used as the fuel for a low-wage economy. If these dangers are to be addressed, policy-makers must focus on the economic engine that is driving the immigration, and the public must be prepared to pay the costs.

If we choose not to pay more now for the work performed by the pover-ty-level work force, then we should realize we will merely pay in the future for the costs of the human ruin created by the existence of that work force. Specifically, what can be done?

The U.S. economy's demand for low-wage labor has risen fast for the past twenty years at least, but the supply has risen even faster. As a result, the relative status of that labor force has declined. This is not, however, merely a product of market forces; very little in the U.S. economy is determined by the market alone. The condition of the low-wage labor force reflects government policy, even if that policy has been to simply ignore the situation.

Federal, state, and local governments have many tools to regulate the condition of labor in U.S. society. These include but are not limited to the minimum wage, worker safety standards, rules governing labor relations (espe-cially union organizing), the collection of employee taxes, and sanctions against the employment of illegal aliens. A determined, systematic, long-term effort on all these fronts could gradually improve the wages and working con-ditions of the poverty-level work force by bringing a greater number of jobs into compliance with the law. The initiative does need to be brusque. Indeed, that would not be feasible, politically or practically. But government at all levels can and should demonstrate through action that it will not tolerate the continual violation of laws at the expense of the most vulnerable people in our society.

Gradually improving the condition of the low-wage work force address-es only one of the challenges posed by the current wave of immigration. At the same time, society must decide what kinds of services, especially in education, it is willing to offer new immigrants and their children in order to enhance their prospects for upward mobility. During 1994, this issue has arisen most forcefully in California.

CHAPTER 12

DEBATING THE COSTS OF IMMIGRATION

It seems almost pedestrian to argue that every U.S. citizen has a stake in making immigration a success. One would think the downside was obvious. Allow a million people a year into the country, sit back and watch while a fifth or a quarter or a third of them fail, and after a decade or two you've got quite a substantial problem. But even now, well into the second decade of the current wave of immigration, there is no widespread feeling that the process of bringing foreign-born people into U.S. society should somehow involve a communal civic responsibility and a basic national interest.

Take for example the role of the federal government. Throughout the agricultural and industrial waves of migration from the late eighteenth to the early twentieth centuries, the government did little more than count people as they came in. Sometimes it did not even do that. For the past century or so, ever since the era of free immigration ended, the government has served chiefly as a gatekeeper and little else. Immigration policy is no more than an effort to regulate who comes into the country. It has little to say about what happens to them once they are here.

This approach is based on the notion that once immigrants are admitted into the country, they are basically on their own to succeed or fail. Families, employers, and others who sponsor immigrants are technically responsible for their welfare for a few years. Otherwise, as far as Washington is concerned, they merit no special consideration. In general, the American mainstream has gone along with this attitude, washing its hands of taking any care of newcomers. (Refugees from Communist countries have been the one exception to this rule, often receiving generous resettlement assistance from both private charities and the government.)

The unspoken premise is that the strong ones will prosper here, and those who don't should not become public burdens. Or as the thought manifests itself in the minds of a great many people, "My grandfather arrived with nothing more than a cardboard suitcase. No one gave him anything he didn't earn, so why should we have to help these people coming now?"

This is a vestige of social Darwinism, and is based on an idea of government that is obsolete. Arguing that government has no place in ensuring the success of immigration is the equivalent of arguing that the government has no role in ensuring safe working conditions, providing secure income for old people, or guaranteeing the solvency of banks. Government didn't do any of those things during the last wave of immigration, which ended in the 1920s. Indeed, many immigrants of the last wave worked in dangerous factories, went into retirement with no Social Security, and saw all their savings wiped out by the bank failures of the Great Depression.

In this regard the great historical change that lies between the last wave of immigration and the current one involves a change in the quality of government. It is absurd to argue that immigrants should make it on their own today—no one in U.S. society makes it on their own. The key difference between the 1920s and the 1990s is that, for better or worse, government now plays a much more active role now in every aspect of life, from the workplace to the schoolhouse to the emergency room. Government has helped build a civic infrastructure, and it provides an extensive social safety net. For the most part all of this developed after the last wave of immigration ended.

As a result, we have no ideological basis for defining the relationship between immigrants and the institutions that oversee the social welfare of this country. This means we have no satisfactory way of defining where and how immigrants fit into our society. It is a disconnection with grave consequences; for example, heightening the anxiety surrounding the politics of immigration and thereby opening the door to nativism. Ultimately, it prevents us from seeing any national purpose in immigration.

THE CALIFORNIA FAULT LINE

These fault lines are now painfully evident in a vigorous political debate that has fundamentally redefined the immigration issue by making it a matter of fiscal policy. As with so many political trends, this one began in California and then swept across the country before seizing a place in the Washington agenda.

With Governor Pete Wilson in the lead, California's elected officials from both parties have proposed a variety of measures based on the idea that immigration, especially illegal immigration, has contributed to the state's large budget deficit. For example, the state enacted a law demanding that applicants for a driver's license show proof of their legal immigration status, and San Diego County stopped reimbursing hospitals for medical care given to undocumented patients.

Supporters of these measures argue that illegal aliens consume more in government services than they pay in taxes, and they contend that the federal government should make up this alleged shortfall because controlling immigration is a federal responsibility. The proponents insist that illegal immigration can be discouraged by denying government services, such as public education, to those who come without authorization. These arguments were first articulated in Sacramento in late 1992, but within a year the theme had been picked up by officials in Florida and New York. By early 1994 the debate had moved to Congress, where these concepts were used to deny long-term earthquake relief to illegal aliens in Los Angeles.

These developments raise four distinct issues:

THE IMMIGRATION ISSUE. Can access to services be manipulated as a tool of immigration policy? Proponents of the new restrictions argue that access to public schools and to publicly supported health care serve as magnets that attract illegal immigration. They claim that fewer people will move to the United States unlawfully if government makes an aggressive effort to prevent illegal immigrants from using these services.

The most frequently cited illustration is the pregnant women who cross the border to take advantage of better obstetric care in U.S. hospitals and additionally to have a child that is a U.S. citizen by birth. No firm data are available to demonstrate the size of the phenomenon. However, years of studies and surveys indicate that the vast majority of illegal migrants are motivated by other factors altogether, such as the need to adjust to changing political and economic circumstances at home, family reunification, the availability of a smoothly working migratory channel, and the prospect of finding work here. (As a practical measure, officials from the Immigration and Naturalization Service all the way up to the commissioner have said it would be prohibitively expensive to check the immigration status of every child entering public school and every indigent hospital patient.)

There is also an unstated supposition behind these proposals—that denying services to illegal aliens might just make them uncomfortable enough to choose to go home. The United States has not engaged in large-scale forced repatriations since the 1950s. But if policymakers or legislators believe that an aggressive policy of removal is now justified, then the issue ought to be debated openly. Otherwise, it is rather unseemly for a nation to deny people education and health care as a backhanded way of chasing them away.

THE FEDERALISM ISSUE. California has led the way among states claiming that illegal immigration poses an unfair fiscal burden that Washington must relieve. Federal mandates prevent states from using immigration status to deny people certain services, chiefly emergency health care and public education. Nevertheless, Florida, California, and Texas have filed lawsuits to get federal reimbursement for state and local expenses on immigrants, based on the contention that the federal government controls immigration policy and therefore should bear the costs.

Although the size of the fiscal burden, especially as regards illegal immigrants, is subject to widely conflicting statistics, the states are basing their claims on a widely accepted principle. Congress has repeatedly recognized that an influx of immigrants can pose an undue fiscal burden on state and local governments. Programs have been authorized to provide funds for the resettlement of refugees and the costs associated with applicants to the 1986 amnesty program and the incarceration of Mariel refugees, although on several occasions actual funds were not appropriated for these programs.

The current wave of immigrants has tended to settle in a few big cities, which are consequently obliged to pay extra costs for everything from bilingual education to court translators. Immigrants meanwhile, like all other taxpayers, render the largest share of their tax payments to the federal government. The costs are local, the benefits national. Given the political importance of the states most forcefully pressing such claims, the Clinton administration has already indicated that it will try to devise a palliative.

THE POLITICAL ISSUE. In an open letter to President Clinton published as a full-page newspaper advertisement in July 1993, California's governor Pete Wilson called for a constitutional change in the qualifications for citizenship so that the children of illegal immigrants would not automatically become U.S. citizens when born here. This proposal highlighted a key issue: What is the definition of citizenship in the modern world? And does it go beyond mere allegiance to a flag to include access to government services, as is already the case in European welfare states? Are there in fact different degrees of citizenship, allowing access to some benefits at some levels and not at others? And what are the standards for inclusion, and who sets them? The answers to these questions will not only define the United States' place in a world of migrants, but also set the ground rules for the nation as a political community.

Governor Wilson's proposal would require a constitutional amendment, and that is the proper level of gravity that it merits. This new wave of immigration should prompt a discussion of how Americans define the standards for admission into their civic society in the broadest terms, not just the formal granting of citizenship. In the past, participation and responsibility have been determined on the basis of presence. A person living in a given jurisdiction pays property taxes, sales taxes, and other levies regardless of whether they are a citizen or an illegal alien. In exchange, they get the right to a variety of benefits. If this social contract is still valid, it deserves to be reaffirmed. If not, the nation needs to find an alternative.

THE INTEGRATION ISSUE. The decision as to whether the United States wants to help ensure the success of the newly arrived must now be made in the midst of a great wave of immigration. The country must decide how much it is willing to spend on providing medical care to immigrants and educating their children, and what it can ask of them in return.

REDEFINING CITIZENSHIP

Despite John F. Kennedy's "ask not" dictum, membership in U.S. civic society is increasingly defined by the services individuals receive from the state rather than the allegiances or services they render their country. The complaints posed by California and other states over the fiscal costs of immigration starkly highlight the connection between the status of individuals in society and their right to services. By scrutinizing the newcomers' access to social service, politicians are not merely searching for budget cuts; they are redefining the concept of citizenship.

Although illegal migrants are the ostensible targets of the budget cutters, legal immigrants have become targets as well. In 1993 Congress extended the period of time a legal immigrant must reside in the United States before becoming eligible for welfare benefits, and further restrictions are expected as part of the welfare reform effort this year.

In the end, the debate over services to immigrants legal or illegal is about the kind of status American society affords newcomers. They will be categorized as deserving of society's help through government or not. This decision defines membership in civic society in ways that go far beyond the specific programs in question. When Congress decided in February 1994 to block illegal aliens in Los Angeles from receiving long-term earthquake relief, it necessarily conveyed a value judgment about their place in the United States. Even though they were as needy as other victims of this natural disaster, Congress defined the migrants as unworthy of help on the basis of their immigration status. In other words, humanitarian concerns were superseded by a compulsion to limit the immigrants' access to government help.

In making their claims on federal funds for the costs of illegal immigration, the states of California and Florida have engaged in a novel sort of human ledger-keeping. They have attempted to separate illegal aliens from other residents as an accounting matter, and have then subjected the migrants to a unique cost-benefit analysis. The migrants' estimated tax contributions were weighed against the estimated value of all the services they receive. Perhaps for the first time in U.S. history there was an effort to assign an actual dollar value to a group's participation in civil society.

This exercise was necessary so that the states could demand a specific amount of money from Washington. It would not have worked to claim simply that providing services to illegal immigrants was just another unfunded federal mandate, like making public buildings accessible to the disabled. After all, illegal immigrants represent revenue as well as expenditures. They pay sales taxes at the cash register and property taxes through rent and even some income taxes. Needless to say, the states have concluded that illegal immigrants are, ultimately, a net loss.

Their estimates, however, were based on very skimpy data and very general assumptions. Conclusions about the earnings and tax payments of illegal immigrants were sometimes based on surveys involving fewer than fifty people. All the specific numbers are in dispute. But the numbers are far less important than the principles involved.

At one level, the California and Florida initiatives suggest that the population can be divided into two classes of citizens: those deserving of government services and those who are undeserving based on their net contributions to the public coffer. This idea of evaluating individuals as fiscal assets or debits runs directly counter to the democratic ideal of government as a collective responsibility operated for the collective good. If individual accounting becomes acceptable, such logic would ultimately call on people with many children to pay more taxes, not less, and for the elderly to be cut off from Social Security as soon as they collected more than the value of their personal contributions.

At another level, the states' initiative suggests that membership in society—citizenship in its broadest sense—should require society's consent. Because illegal aliens lack that consent, the argument goes, they can be denied access to services reserved for members. Since last year, illegal immigrants in California have been denied driver's licenses, an important measure of membership. This argument has some clear precedents. Prior to the enactment of the Fourteenth Amendment to the Constitution, which opened citizenship to all persons born in the United States regardless of their origins, American society found it perfectly acceptable to deny citizenship to Native Americans and people born as slaves.

The key issue here involves society's consent. Technically, but only technically, the federal government does not consent to the presence of illegal immigrants in this country. As a practical matter, of course, it does little to keep them out. Otherwise, the undocumented aliens receive plenty of de facto consent to their presence in this country. They get consent everyday from their employers, their customers, and their landlords, among others. Congress offered a degree of consent when it enacted an amnesty for illegal aliens who had lived in the United States for several years or who had contributed by doing seasonal agricultural work. So just how illegal are the illegals? And in whose eyes are they illegal?

Under the U.S. social welfare system, benefits are bestowed on the basis of need, not in proportion to the size of tax payments. Current federal law holds that immigration status cannot be used to determine eligibility for education and health programs. The immigration backlash rising out of California is challenging both of these principles, and the challenges are likely to soon end up before the U.S. Supreme Court.

In many ways the questions raised by Governor Wilson have the potential to generate a much-needed debate. Even his foes should welcome him as a provocateur. As difficult as the issue may seem, the United States must decide how the new migrants will relate to the national society before the current wave of immigration proceeds much further. This is the issue Governor Wilson has forced onto the national agenda.

CHAPTER 13

TOWARD A POLICY OF INTEGRATION

Before the debate over the Clinton administration's proposal for universal health care is finished, immigration will be discussed in a way it never has been. Illegal immigrants almost certainly will be excluded from the coverage, but at what level? Will children have to prove their legal status before receiving vaccinations? Will people with non-life-threatening illnesses simply be turned away from clinics and hospitals? The issues will be no simpler when legal immigrants are involved. At what stage do they qualify for that health security card? The day they arrive? When they get a job? After a year? Three years? Five? Are they covered if their immigration status is in dispute? Will applicants for political asylum get coverage automatically, or only after their claims have been heard by a judge?

As a technical matter, the issue can be debated piecemeal, program by program: Illegal immigrants can get emergency help in a natural disaster, but for how long? If a citizen sponsors an elderly parent as a legal immigrant, when can the parents qualify for Medicaid? But this approach does little to solve the overall dilemma. Since mid-1993 Congress and several state legislatures have focused on these kinds of details, but they have left unanswered the much broader and more fundamental questions that arise from the need to integrate immigrants in a civic society that revolves around state control of social services.

A true policy of integration would create a framework for resolving all these individual disputes. Such a policy would define the nation's interests in immigration and the means it would pursue to achieve these interests. Such a policy would define what services and benefits newcomers would receive to ease their way in the United States, and what would be expected of them in return.

101

It is important to remember that the current wave of immigration occurred after the existing structure of services and benefits had been erected; such an influx of foreigners was never a major concern when the political foundation for that structure was created. A policy of integration would therefore necessarily involve adapting these government structures and political concepts to new purposes, one of the most difficult feats to achieve in a democracy.

This process of adaptation will be all the more difficult because of the way the politics of entitlement have developed in recent years. Having created a much larger government for themselves during a time of low immigration, Americans began a revolt against the size and costs of this government at about the same time the latest wave of immigration began. Indeed, even if most of the new immigrants were from Europe, there would still be controversy over their access to government services because the dimensions of those ser-vices and the costs of government have risen so much since the last major wave of immigration ended in the 1920s. Now with the wave in full flow, the political priority is to reduce government spending at all levels.

The issue is all the more contentious because much of the logic behind the various social welfare programs evolved out of the civil rights era. Some programs were specifically meant as responses to the needs of groups who in the past had been denied full membership in society. Others were based simply on current expressions of need. Taken together, the constellation of civil rights, antipoverty, and equal-opportunity initiatives created a new category of people with a special claim on government services: the minority group. This in effect established a new level of citizenship, made up of those who deserved special services because they had been denied full membership in the past.

By virtue of nationality or ethnicity or race, most immigrants today can be put in this category even if they do not have historical grievances against American society. However, immigrants often end up with a weaker claim on government precisely because they are identified with a demanding and expen-sive minority group. As the pendulum has swung against increased spending, it has also swung against special consideration for ethnic and racial groups. The special status that comes with membership in a minority group now opens people to disparagement as well as privilege.

BILINGUAL EDUCATION: LEARNING AS AN ENTITLEMENT PROGRAM

The challenge of developing a policy of integration that jibes with the politics of entitlement is clearest in the area of public education, especially in the sad and difficult history of bilingual education. Throughout most of the first and second waves of immigration, many public and parochial schools taught immigrant children in their native languages. This was especially true among nationalities like the Germans, who fought to maintain their heritage. By 1900 about 4 percent of the elementary-school population, more than 600,000 children, received all or part of their instruction in German. The practice generally died out during the wave of nativism that swept the country after the turn of the century and again during World War I.

Teaching in a language other than English was revived in Florida after the initial Cuban exodus in 1959. Once again, the practice was strictly related to immigration. Bilingual education blossomed into a national phenomenon only in the 1960s, when it was detached from immigration and became a civil rights matter. Indeed, the Bilingual Education Act of 1968 was envisioned as a Great Society program to help students who were both poor and "educationally disadvantaged because of their inability to speak English." In 1974, the U.S. Supreme Court's landmark ruling in *Lau v. Nichols* applied to bilingual education the same logic already used to strike down racially "separate but equal" schools. It ruled that providing instruction only in English denied equal access to education for children who do not speak English well.[1]

Both the 1968 law and the 1974 court decision shared two characteristics that have set the terms for virtually all subsequent discussion of bilingual education. Both put bilingual education within that nexus of civil rights and social disadvantage that constitutes minority group grievances. And neither dictated what kind of instruction would adequately redress that grievance.

As a result, the very idea of bilingual education, let alone its funding, was left exposed to ideological attack by those who opposed social welfare programs in principle. The well-intentioned design of letting local authorities devise the best bilingual instruction for their own students resulted in pedagogical cacophony. There are so many different classroom approaches and so little agreement on what works that proponents of bilingual education have been unable to provide the public with the kind of clear, comprehensible rationale that creates political support for a program.

As recent studies by the Rand Corporation and the Urban Institute have shown, the federal government has basically dropped out of bilingual education and virtually all other forms of funding for education aimed at immigrants.[2] From 1981 to 1991, while the greatest influx of immigrants since the 1920s was taking place, federal funding for bilingual education was cut in half in real dollars, with annual spending falling to a level of between $175 to $200 million. An emergency immigrant education fund program was also gutted and the only program aimed at refugee children was eliminated. Moreover, even though immigrant children increasingly fit the qualification of poverty and low achievement, the Urban Institute found that children who needed help learning English were often excluded from federally funded programs for needy students.

Not only has bilingual education failed to attract support with the increase in immigration, but the influx of people has actually prompted a new assault. During the 1980s the most visible response to the growing numbers of immigrants in the schools was the move to kill bilingual education altogether and to mandate English as an official language. Achieving notable success at the state and local levels, "English-only" activists allege that today's immigrants will Balkanize the nation, and bilingual education is painted as a kind of subversive expression of ethnicity.

Except for a few holdouts among the most rabid restrictionists, the official English movement collapsed for a variety of reasons, among them the fact that the threat of linguistic separatism never materialized. To the contrary, all evidence shows that immigrants, especially the young, are learning English with remarkable speed.

The 1990 census counted some 6.3 million school-age children living in households where a language other than English was spoken, 14 percent of the total population in that age group. Of these, nearly 4 million were found to speak English "very well." Even taking into account the young people who have had the least opportunity to learn English—school-age immigrants who entered the country in the 1980s—more than half speak English very well.

Clearly the children of immigrant households are adapting linguistically at a rapid pace, and it seems a simple proposition to argue that society has a self-interest in helping them. Indeed, it is evident that on this matter, at least the momentum is already going in the right direction, unlike so many other social issues. All that is needed for further adaptation by immigrant children is some encouragement. But spending significant federal tax dollars on the education of immigrants will not become politically viable unless there is a fundamental redefinition of the immigrant's position in U.S. society.

FROM MINORITIES TO NEWCOMERS

In order to accomplish this redefinition of the immigrants' place in the United States, it will be important to view immigration as a pressing social issue of the 1990s, not as a leftover from the agenda of the 1960s. Given the numbers of newcomers, immigration deserves a contemporary policy response based on a fresh analysis of both its contributions to society, and its costs. But before immigration gets this fresh look it deserves, policymakers will have to clear away the mines left over from past battles.

Returning to the example of bilingual education, new programs for educating immigrant children need not be viewed as compensation for the grievances that the native-born students hold against U.S. society. Native-born Latinos will continue to seek social justice where they believe it has been denied to them, as well they should. But their struggle should not automatically become identified with the needs of new immigrants. At the same time, policymakers must not assume that by addressing the needs of immigrants they have somehow resolved all the issues that arise from the historical position of native-born Latinos as a minority group in the United States. The history of the nonimmigrant Latino population in the United States should provide the backdrop for developing a new policy of integration, and if that policy is successful the new generation of immigrant Latinos will write its own history.

The 1990 census found more than two million school-age children who to some extent or another have not mastered English, about 5 percent of the total. Some are newly arrived, and some are children born here of the newly arrived. Others are born into long-standing Latino communities that have maintained their linguistic identity. But no matter where they come from, during a time of immigration it can be assumed this sector of the population will be constantly replenished. What is important is that a majority of these children who have not mastered English are native-born U.S. citizens, and almost all are expected to live here to adulthood.

Regardless of the origins of the students who do not yet speak English well, every bit of available evidence shows three common characteristics among them:

- They are in the process of learning English simply by virtue of being in this country, and the only real issue is how much English they will learn by adulthood.

- They will learn English and all other subjects best if most of their education is addressed to them in a language they understand, especially when they first enter U.S. schools.

- Those who master English will stay in school longer, go on to earn more money at work, and bear children who are also more likely to enjoy upward mobility. These characteristics, in turn, will greatly reduce the chance these children or their offspring will become dangers to society or dependent on welfare programs.

It appears that spending money to aid the education of children still learning English is a long-term investment for society, with a very high probability of substantial payoff. The rationale need be no more complicated than that. If public education meets its responsibilities to these students, they will be more productive workers and better citizens. Everyone wins.

The entire proposition looks very different when it is cast in terms of educating a work force rather than as compensation to the disadvantaged. At a time of immigration it seems almost self-evident that society has an interest in schooling newcomers, especially young people, especially to master English, even if that means having to invest extra resources in them. But the goal must be stated in extremely pragmatic terms that emphasize the benefits to society—for example, more productive workers and better citizens—while perhaps deemphasizing the concept of an immigrant's "right" to the benefits. On this basis it might be possible to generate ongoing political support for something that would look and act like bilingual education but would have to be known by some less controversial name.

The key to achieving such a consensus lies in an accurate and credible definition of the way immigration functions in our society. Immigration of some magnitude is unavoidable, so it should be viewed as a national enterprise in which everyone shares the risks and potential benefits. Immigration helps meet our economy's demand for new workers. It helps define our place in the world. Everyone therefore has a stake in making it more successful even if that means an up-front investment of money in the newcomers.

If immigration is posed on those terms, it then becomes fair to ask about the flip side of the transaction. What do the immigrants bring to the enterprise? And what can be asked of them in exchange for the benefits they draw?

THE IMMIGRATION CONTRACT

The concept at the heart of an integration policy is that immigration involves a kind of contract between the receiving nation and the newcomers. Immigrants have always brought along a variety of assets both tangible and intangible. Years of education paid for elsewhere, dynamism, diversity, and hard cash are among these assets. In exchange, the United States has offered intangible benefits, such as political freedom and economic opportunity, as well as more concrete services, such as a decent education system.

In the immigration contract both sides put assets on the table and assume risks. For the nation, the goal of this bargain is to maximize the immigrants' potential contributions. For the immigrant, the goal is have the greatest possible opportunity to flourish here. The immigration contract starts from the assumption that these goals are fundamentally compatible, and it then assigns rights and responsibilities to each side.

But even though the United States is experiencing historically high levels of immigration, it has no functioning contract with the newcomers. There is no consensus over what the nation should do to help immigrants and what can be expected of them in return. This is painfully obvious in the debate initiated by Governor Wilson's proposals to reduce immigrants' access to government programs. The ultimate goal of those proposals is not to make immigration more effective but simply to reduce the number of newcomers, especially the number of those living here illegally. Other proposals would cut the number of legal immigrants. But successful integration is not simply a matter of numbers. No matter how much the nation restricts immigration, it must take steps to ensure that those who are admitted become successful members of U.S. society.

During the last wave of immigration this contract was largely implicit. Market forces and a host of private institutions, churches, charities, and political parties were left to carry out the bargain. Government now plays a much larger role in U.S. society than it did a hundred years ago, and hence a much larger role in executing the contract between the newcomers and their new society. This is most clearly evident in the complex infrastructure of educational and social welfare institutions that government has created since the end of the last big wave of European immigration.

In order to produce successful integration, any new contract between the United States and its immigrants is certain to involve the delivery of government services, especially education and health care. This requires a politically viable rationale for spending public funds on people not born here. Appeals to humanitarian ideals alone will not produce steady appropriations. Given the fiscal perceptions that have come to guide decisionmaking, this means there must be a consensus that immigrants somehow compensate society for those expenditures.

The traditional view of this compensation is that immigrants bring to the United States a variety of assets both tangible and intangible—the years of education paid for elsewhere (since most immigrants arrive as adults), their dynamism, and, often, hard cash. Also, every once in a while a genius slips in among them—not that the United States screens immigrants to get a good selection. Instead, traditionally, it has relied on an immigration system based on family reunification and employer preferences. Therefore, most immigrants have fulfilled some sort of need here. And, traditionally, immigrants have arrived with a built-in support system to help them get settled, since their sponsors must offer formal assurances that the newcomers will not become public charges, at least in the first few years they are here.

This traditional view remains valid for most immigrants, and certainly for an overwhelming majority of those who arrive legally. But recently it has lost much of its persuasive power as the many illegal aliens in the current flow are perceived as abusing the openness of the United States. The traditional view is also challenged by the misperception that the 18 percent of all immigrants now living in poverty have more of an impact on U.S. society than the vast majority who prosper here. And the view is challenged by the realization that the influx includes growing numbers of refugees and asylum seekers who have great needs but who do not necessarily have families or jobs to welcome them. Finally, the traditional view of immigrants is challenged by the fact so many of the new arrivals are of racial groups that in the past have not been part of mainstream American society.

Given these realities it is evident that any successful policy of integration will have to be based on a reevaluation of the assets that immigrants bring to their new society. As a first step, those assets need to be understood in terms of the dynamics of contemporary immigration:

THE FACE OF CHANGE. Immigration is the inevitable result of change in economic and political structures around the world. The human flow includes people leaving Third World nations that are undergoing painful economic transitions, and it includes many fleeing political upheaval. Therefore, the nature of these flows is that they often include people who will break the law in order to migrate.

Consider the kinds of changes that have been taking place recently—the end of the Cold War, the rise of market economies in Latin America, the globalization of American culture. Without question, the United States has been by far the largest beneficiary of these changes. Meanwhile, it has received a fairly small portion of all the people displaced by those changes. On a global scale, immigration is a bargain for the United States.

THE UNITED STATES AS INSTIGATOR. Policymakers and the public must bear in mind that the immigrants are not the only active party in this event. The United States is not merely a passive and receiving society. Instead, both the U.S. government and society help establish migration channels and actively attract immigrants for both political and economic reasons. Moreover, immigrants fill a demand created by a congruence of demographic and economic trends in the United States. Hence, an added asset for the immigrants is that their arrival responds to the needs of the United States. It is a product, albeit sometimes unintended, of U.S. initiatives.

A MATURING MIGRATION. The current wave of migration has been under way for almost thirty years, and soon a decade will have passed since the big numbers of Latinos and Asians began arriving in the 1980s. Most are now settled and have begun raising families. A vast generation of young people, the children of these immigrants, is now making its way into the public school system. They are U.S. citizens for the most part, and almost all are certain to remain here. Even if all new immigration were shut off tomorrow, the children of immigrants already here would still play a key role in the twenty-first century labor force.

RIGHTS OF ACCESS

Even after adding up all these factors, there are still unresolved questions regarding government services to immigrants. The issue need not be posed in transactional terms, as it has been during the fiscal backlash of the past year; that is, do immigrants contribute a dollar in taxes for every dollar of services they use? Instead, the issue can be framed as one of access, or, more precisely, rights of access, and the benefits society gains by granting that access.

For the great majority of contemporary immigrants, the education, health, and social welfare systems they encounter here are far superior to the ones they leave behind in their native lands. This does not mean that social infrastructure is what draws them here or that they make extraordinary use of it once they arrive. On both counts, the evidence points to opposite conclusions. Once immigrants are settled, like any other of the United States taxpayers, they contribute to the current costs and future expansion of that infrastructure. But the fact remains that on arrival immigrants encounter a preexisting network of services that they did not help create. Admission to the country implies some degree of access to that system.

It is on this score that immigration policy has lagged behind developments in domestic policy. Immigrants' access to welfare or health care received little attention until the anti-immigrant backlash in California transformed it into an explosive issue. Since then, the focus has been on cutting benefits for people already in the country, a response that has provoked tremendous anxiety and defensiveness in Latino communities.

Instead of launching retroactive measures that have a punitive effect on people already in the country, policymakers should undertake a full review of the eligibility rules for the whole range of social welfare programs. Any decision to restrict the access of noncitizens should be applied only to new incoming migrants, but not to those who arrived in the United States under another set of assumptions. Such a review must be conducted with the goals of immigration policy in mind, not just an urge to cut the budget. In particular, the goal of successful integration of immigrants should be in the forefront. These two goals, budget cutting and the successful integration of immigrants, often, however, appear to be mutually exclusive.

Policymakers should never lose sight of what happens to the concept of citizenship under these pressures to cut the budget. Every measure that reduces benefits to noncitizens creates a financial incentive for immigrants to seek citizenship. Somehow it seems contrary to American ideals for people to swear allegiance to the Constitution solely as a way to get access to food stamps or health care.

Second, policymakers should consider what happens to immigrants who have no access to public services such as welfare or long-term hospital care. Will they pack up and go home to face an even less certain fate? Not likely. Will the government begin deporting immigrants because they are poor? Less likely. Instead, needy immigrants cut off from access to social welfare programs and their offspring will be relegated to a second-class status with little chance of successful integration. In this regard immigrants are no different from the native born. The goal of social welfare programs should be to move them toward independence and not to create more expensive forms of dependence in the future. By adjusting the rules of access for future immigrants, policymakers can reduce the costs of social services to immigrants while still promoting successful integration.

At the very heart of U.S. immigration policy is the idea that the families who sponsor newcomers must take financial responsibility for them, at least for a while. This is the most explicit immigration contract. In 1993 Congress extended the period of sponsorship from three years to five years. If an immigrant applies for welfare-type benefits during that time, the sponsor's income is factored into the decision on eligibility. This period could easily be extended in certain immigrant categories. For siblings and adult children, the sponsorship period could go to ten years, for example. That would go beyond the time when the immigrant has become eligible for citizenship, and indeed the sponsorship should continue even after a person naturalizes. The sponsorship is a condition of entry, and it should remain with an immigrant regardless of other changes in the person's status.

Aside from restricting access to entitlement programs, the government could enforce the sponsorship with the kind of measures now being applied to child support. If someone sponsors a sibling and fails to take financial responsibility for the immigrant, the government could attach the sponsor's wages.

The most tempting budgetary target—parents sponsored by their adult children who have become U.S. citizens—are a special case that may require some simple compassion. These immigrants arrive at the end of their working lives and have no chance to build up Social Security benefits or to qualify for health insurance. Caring for an elderly relative without insurance or Medicaid or Medicare can bankrupt even a successful middle-class family. This seems an extraordinary burden to put on an immigrant already attempting to fulfill the most basic human responsibilities to care for parents. Yet this expensive category of immigrant is certain to grow as the current wave of migration matures.

In summation, three principles should be observed in order to preserve the goal of successful integration:

- Instead of changing the rules in mid-game for immigrants already here, restrictions should apply only to future immigrants.

- Access to services should not be tied to citizenship.

- The safety net should be made available when both the immigrant and the sponsor fall on hard times.

Also, policymakers could consider imposing a substantial one-time tax on immigrants and/or their sponsors at the moment of entry. This tax would constitute an up-front cash contribution to the social welfare infrastructure and would assure the immigrant access to programs. Such a contribution would be all the more justified if the nation was seriously committed to educating immigrants and offering them health-care guarantees. In effect, the nation would ask immigrants to pay a membership fee for the use of the social welfare infrastructure, and in exchange they would receive an unambiguous welcome.

The challenge would be to make such a tax progressive and fair. People coming to take specific jobs would pay in proportion to their salaries. Refugees and asylum applicants would not pay at all. For family immigrants the tax would fall on the relatives that sponsor them and would be based on the size of their incomes. Immigrants who have become U.S. citizens had an average annual per capita income of $20,538 in 1990, considerably more than the $14,637 averaged by native-born workers, according to the census.[3] Certainly it seems plausible to ask someone to contribute 5 percent of one year's income for the right to come here to take a job or to bring a relative into the country on a permanent basis.

During the 1992 federal fiscal year, 973,977 people would have been subject to such a tax as they gained permanent resident status. With a tax averaging $1,000 a person, the revenue gain would be almost $1 billion. Even in Washington that is serious money. While this tax would not pay for the services immigrants receive on a dollar-for-dollar basis, it would pay for a lot of bilingual teachers, language training for police officers, and the like. At this stage of the immigration debate, the details of such a proposal are less important than the need to focus attention on society's right to make demands of immigrants and its obligation to render the services necessary for their successful integration.

A NEW RELATIONSHIP

Welfare reform, health-care reform, and the backlash against immigrants have all prompted a reexamination of the way immigration fits into the United States infrastructure of public sector benefits and services. The debate over this relationship has already been joined, and now is the time to begin aiming for a successful conclusion. Any serious discussion will surely move public perceptions beyond the idea that immigrants come here to take advantage of the U.S. social welfare system and that they represent a drain on U.S. society. Instead, a new vision of immigration might emerge, a vision of two partners in a mutual undertaking.

Immigrants no longer come as creators of a new society, nor as foreigners free to carve a niche in a growing industrial economy. Instead, today's migrants begin their relationship with the United States long before they leave home. They travel here along routes that also carry America's culture, trade, finance, diplomacy, and other energies across the globe. Once here, they are categorized by the degree of membership they will enjoy in American civil society and in the level of government benefits they are entitled to receive.

Any decision to cut off any substantial group of migrants from the social infrastructure ultimately dooms them, or more likely their children, to lives of poverty, failure, and the potential for much greater dependency in the future. Worse yet is when illegal aliens are members of minority groups, a category that has become the whipping boy of the immigrant backlash. In this state of ultimate exclusion, the individual is granted no right to exist as a recognized civic entity yet is accorded the privilege of feeling a historic grievance against society. No nation can conduct large-scale immigration successfully based on degrees of exclusion.

Immigration should be viewed as an enterprise in which both the immigrant and the host nation bring certain assets to the table and both have an interest in seeing that the enterprise succeeds. Both sides must make investments in each other, and both take risks on the assumption that they will each draw returns. From that starting point the almost inevitable conclusion is a policy of integration that makes the best possible use of the assets that the immigrant and the host society bring together. The newcomers should be welcomed with membership in society based on family ties, their direct contributions to the public coffers, their willingness to work, and society's need for their labor. Providing bilingual education for the immigrants' children is therefore a matter of the host society's self-interest. The same would be true of many other initiatives, including low-cost English classes for adult immigrants, the ready availability of interpreters in public offices, and a determined effort to convince all eligible immigrants to become citizens.

Above all, a policy of integration would guarantee that immigrants working for low wages are treated decently and not as objects of exploitation. Such a policy of integration could do a great deal to quell the dangers so evident when Latino immigrants have taken to the streets of Los Angeles, New York, and Washington. Rather than merely add 200,000 or 300,000 or 400,000 new candidates to the underclass every year, society would set out to work with immigrants and thus ensure a better result.

The large and growing population of illegal immigrants stands as an unsurpassable barrier to any such policy of integration, and the need for such a policy is the best argument for efforts to address the illegal influx. No political consensus granting immigrants real membership in American society is possible so long as citizens suspect they are being cheated by people who have sneaked across the border. Equally important, no effort to improve the status of the low-wage work force can succeed so long as hiring illegal aliens gives employers an escape hatch from the laws designed to protect American workers.

As the long history of Mexican migration has proven, however, this problem cannot be solved by deportations, border fences, or other law enforcement measures aimed at the illegal migrants. Perhaps the best alternative lies in a policy that has achieved widespread support at least in part, but that has never been implemented: a determined assault on jobs that fail to meet the legal standards of decent employment.

All of this involves painful, sometimes expensive choices. In this regard immigration is not unlike deficit spending. It is very easy to avoid the hard choices, especially in economic good times, because there is no evident pain. But the longer the reckoning is put off, the more it hurts, especially in hard times. All of the above is also true of the United States' splurge on poverty-level laborers, as now the nation faces a very large social deficit in the form of people who must work very hard to live just this side of indigence.

Nations have relatively few means by which to expand their populations. They can conquer or colonize other peoples. They can grow through natural increase. Or they can accept immigrants. This latter option is the only one being exercised to any significant degree in the United States today.

Immigrants are a form of progeny, and establishing their place in society will be one of the nation's basic tasks for decades to come. And as was the case with every previous wave of immigrants, it will change the country once again. We will not really know the outcome of that change for twenty or thirty years or longer, but policymakers will set the direction with the decisions they face now.

NOTES

CHAPTER 1

1. Sharon Stanton Russell and Michael S. Teitelbaum, "International Migration and International Trade" Discussion Papers no. 160, World Bank, Washington, D.C., 1992.

2. For a survey of global migration trends, their causes and consequences, see the United Nations Population Fund annual report on the State of the World Population for 1993: *The Individual and the World: Population, Migration and Development in the 1990's* (New York, 1993).

3. Ibid., p. 7.

4. Ibid., p. 8.

CHAPTER 2

1. William S. Bernard, "History of U.S. Immigration Policy," in *Harvard Encyclopedia of American Ethnic Groups*, ed. Stephan Thernstrom et al. (Cambridge, Mass.: Harvard University Press, 1980).

2. U.S. General Accounting Office, *Illegal Aliens: Despite Data Limitations, Current Methods Provide Better Population Estimates*, Report PEMD-93-25, Washington D.C., 1993. Estimates provided by Robert Warren, chief of the statistics branch, Immigration and Naturalization Service.

CHAPTER 3

1. John Higham, *Send These to Me: Immigrants in Urban America* (Baltimore: Johns Hopkins University Press, 1984), p. 21.

2. Ibid., p. 21.

3. Ibid., p. 6.

4. Ibid., p. 31.

CHAPTER 4

1. John Bodnar, *The Transplanted: A History of Immigrants in Urban America* (Bloomington, Ind.: Indiana University Press, 1985), p. 3.

2. Ibid., p. 6.

3. Comprehensive Adult Student Assessment System, *A Survey of Newly Legalized Persons in California* (California Health and Welfare Agency, 1989).

4. Wayne A. Cornelius, "Los Migrantes de la Crisis: The Changing Profile of Mexican Labor Migration to California in the 1980's" (Unpublished paper, Center for U.S.-Mexican Studies, University of California, San Diego, 1989).

CHAPTER 5

1. The findings of some of the major surveys can be found in the following: Wayne A. Cornelius, "Labor Migration to the United States: Development Outcomes and Alternatives in Mexican Sending Communities," Final Report to the Commission for the Study of International Migration and Cooperative Economic Development, Center for U.S.-Mexican Studies, University of California, San Diego, 1990; J. Edward Taylor, "U.S. Immigration Policy and the Mexican Economy," Urban Institute, Washington, D.C., 1988; Alejandro Portes and Robert L. Bach, *Latin Journey* (Berkeley: University of California Press, 1985).

2. Cornelius, "Labor Migration to the United States," p. 35.

3. Glenn Hendricks, *The Dominican Diaspora: From the Dominican Republic to New York City—Villagers in Transition* (New York: Teachers College Press, Columbia University, 1974).

4. Oded Stark and J. Edward Taylor, "Relative Deprivation and Migration: Theory, Evidence and Policy Implications," Working Papers Series 656, Policy, Research, and External Affairs Complex, World Bank, Washington, D.C., 1991.

5. Russell and Teitelbaum, "International Migration and International Trade"; *Individual and the World*, pp. ii, 23.

6. Fernando Lozano Ascencio, "Bringing It Back Home: Remittances to Mexico from Migrant Workers in the United States," Monograph Series 37, Center for U.S.-Mexican Studies, University of California, San Diego, 1993.

7. Taylor, "U.S. Immigration Policy and the Mexican Economy," p. 29.

8. Patrick J. Blessing, "The Irish," in *Harvard Encyclopedia of American Ethnic Groups*, ed. Stephan Thernstrom et al. (Cambridge, Mass.: Harvard University Press, 1980).

9. Sherri Grasmuck and Patricia R. Pessar, *Between Two Islands: Dominican International Migration* (Berkeley: University of California Press, 1991).

CHAPTER 6

1. Saskia Sassen, *The Mobility of Labor and Capital: A Study in International Investment and Labor Flow* (Newcastle upon Tyne: Cambridge University Press, 1988), p. 13.

2. Alejandro Portes and Alex Stepick, *City on the Edge: The Transformation of Miami* (Berkeley: University of California Press, 1993), p. 102.

CHAPTER 7

1. Wayne A. Cornelius and Jorge A. Bustamante, eds., *Mexican Migration to the United States: Origins, Consequences and Policy Options* (San Diego: Center for U.S.-Mexican Studies, University of California, San Diego, 1989); Rodolfo O. de la Garza et al., *The Mexican American Experience: An Interdisciplinary Anthology* (Austin: University of Texas Press, 1987); Ricardo Romo, *East Los Angeles: History of a Barrio* (Austin: University of Texas Press, 1983).

2. Rebecca Morales and Paul M. Ong, "The Illusion of Progress: Latinos in Los Angeles," in Rebecca Morales and Frank Bonilla, eds., *Latinos in a Changing U.S. Economy* (Newberry Park, Calif.: Sage Publications, 1993).

3. U.S. Department of Justice, *Statistical Yearbook of the Immigration and Naturalization Service*, 1992.

4. Cornelius, "Los Migrantes de la Crisis."

CHAPTER 8

1. Doris Meissner, "Managing Migrations," *Foreign Policy*, Spring 1992.

CHAPTER 9

1. Nathan Glazer and Daniel Patrick Moynihan, *Beyond the Melting Pot* (Cambridge, Mass.: MIT Press, 1970).

2. Rodolfo O. de la Garza et al., *Latino Voices: Mexican, Puerto Rican and Cuban Perspectives on American Politics* (Boulder, Colo.: Westview Press, 1992).

CHAPTER 10

1. Tomás Rivera Center, "Latinos and the Los Angeles Uprising: The Economic Context," Claremont, Calif., 1993.

2. Blessing, "The Irish."

3. Raul Hinojosa-Ojeda et al., "An Even Greater 'U-Turn': Latinos and the New Inequality," in *Hispanics in the Labor Force: Issues and Policies*, ed. Edwin Melendez, et al. (New York: Plenum Press, 1991).

4. Saskia Sassen, "Urban Transformation and Unemployment," in Rebecca Morales and Frank Bonilla, eds., *Latinos in a Changing U.S. Economy*,

5. Roger Rouse as quoted in Cornelius, "Los Migrantes de la Crisis," p. 6.

6. Morales and Ong, "Illusion of Progress."

7. Tomás Rivera Center, "Latinos and the Los Angeles Uprising."

8. U.S. Department of Commerce, Bureau of the Census,*The Foreign-Born Population in the United States*, 1990 CP-3-1.

9. Martha Van Haitsma, "Attitudes, Social Context and Labor Force Attachment: Blacks and Immigrant Mexicans in Chicago Poverty Areas" (Paper prepared as part of the Chicago Urban Poverty and Family Structure Project, Chicago, Ill., 1992).

10. Latino Futures Research Group, "Latinos and the Future of Los Angeles," Los Angeles, Latino Coalition, 1993.

11. U.S. Department of Commerce, Bureau of the Census, *Population Projections of the United States, by Age, Sex, Race, and Hispanic Origin: 1993 to 2050*, P25-1104, Washington, D.C., 1993.

12 Alejandro Portes et al., "The Children of Immigrants: The Adaptation Process of the Second Generation" (various publications of a research project still in progress).

CHAPTER 11

1. U.S. General Accounting Office, *Immigration Reform*, March 1990; Frank D. Bean et al., *Undocumented Migration to the United States* (Washington, D.C.: Urban Institute Press, 1990); U.S. Congress, Senate Judiciary Committee, Subcommittee on Immigration and Refugee Affairs, Hearings on the implementation of employer sanctions, April 3 and 10, 1992.

2. Comprehensive Adult Student Assessment System, *A Survey of Newly Legalized Persons in California*.

CHAPTER 13

1. James Crawford, *Bilingual Education: History, Politics, Theory and Practice* (Trenton, N.J.: Crane Publishing, 1989). The history is his, but not the opinions.

2. Michael Fix and Wendy Zimmermann, "Educating Immigrant Children: Chapter 1 in the Changing City," Washington, D.C., Urban Institute, 1993; Lorraine M. McDonnell and Paul T. Hill, *Newcomers in American Schools: Meeting the Educational Needs of Immigrant Youth* (Santa Monica, Calif.: Rand Corporation, 1993).

3. U.S. Department of Commerce, Bureau of the Census,*The Foreign-Born Population in the United States*, 1990 CP-3-1.

INDEX

Acculturation. *See* Assimilation
Africa: emigration from, 3, 59
Afro-Americans. *See* Blacks
Agricultural sector, 13, 48, 54, 87, 89
Amnesty program, 13, 50, 89, 90, 96, 98
Argentina, 45
Asia 43; emigration from, 6, 16, 21, 23, 24, 32
Asian immigrants, 23, 66, 82, 108
Assimilation, 7, 27, 28, 67, 75. *See also* Integration of immigrants
Asylum seekers, 14–16, 45, 58, 107

Baird, Zoe, 88
Bean, Frank D., 67–68
Beginning of migration flow, 42, 43
Beyond the Melting Pot (Glazer and Moynihan), 64
Bilingual education, 102–4, 105–6
Bilingual Education Act (1968), 103
Blacks, 27, 67; economic status, 77, 78, 79, 80; population, 82; residence, 66, 72
Blessing, Patrick J., 40
Bodner, John, 32
Border Patrol (U.S.), 13, 56
Borjas, George J., 81

Bracero program, 13, 21, 33, 48, 49
Brazil, 45

California, 46, 92; economy, 13, 48, 49, 50, 89–90, 94; politics, 69; population, 25, 33, 49; social welfare in, 94–97, 99
Caribbean: emigration from, 6, 15, 37, 40
Carter, Jimmy, 45
Carter administration, 87
Census (1990), 73, 80, 82, 104
Central America: emigration from, 14, 32, 53; relations with United States, 56
Chicago (Ill.), 80
Children of immigrants, 7, 28, 64, 96, 108; education, 83, 102–4, 105; socioeconomic status of, 73–75, 82–83, 85, 86, 112
Chinese immigrants, 15
Cities, 22, 97; conditions in, 7, 25–26, 71–73, 74, 76–77; economy, 49, 69, 73, 77–78, 81, 87; migration to, 75, 96; racial groups in, 66, 72–73, 80–81
Citizenship, 17, 50, 96, 97–98, 109, 110
Civic society: immigrant place in, 96, 97–99, 101, 104, 111–13; Latino place in, 7, 68–69, 80–81

Civil rights, 14, 16, 49, 60, 69–70, 102
Clinton administration, 14–15, 56, 57,
    86, 96, 101
Cold War, 60
Colombian immigrants, 32
Continuation of migration flow, 42, 43–44
Cornelius, Wayne A., 36–37
Cuba, 15, 57–59
Cuban immigrants, 45, 57–58, 59;
    influence of, 25–26, 69, 103; popula-
    tion, 42; status of, 15

DeFreitas, Gregory, 81
Diminution of migration flow, 44, 45,
    48, 50
Dinkins, David, 64
Diversity of immigrants, 23. See also
    Mosaic model;   Multiculturalism
Dominican immigrants, 37, 40, 42, 43,
    72–73, 78
Dominican Republic, 93

Economic development, 54–55
Economic mobility. See Upward mobility
Economic opportunity, 75–76, 106; and
    emigration, 32, 33, 48, 49
Economic refugees, 15
Education, 99; criticism of, 69, 76, 85;
    of immigrant children, 83, 85,
    102–4, 105; of immigrants, 110–11,
    112; level of immigrants, 35, 80, 106
Ellis Island: exhibit, 3–4, 6
El Salvador, 14, 56, 57. See also
    Salvadoran immigrants
Emigrants, 24. See also Immigrants
Emigration: causes, 31–32, 44, 48,
    49–50, 75, 108; goals, 36; reducing,
    34, 40, 54–60. See also Emigration
    under countries and regions, e.g. ,
    Latin America, emigration from
Employer sanctions, 87–88; effective-
    ness of, 13–14, 88–92

Employment, 33, 35, 37, 49, 50, 54, 76,
    112–13; of illegal immigrants, 13–14,
    86, 87–92, 107, 112. See also Labor
    demand; Low-wage labor
English language: and immigrants, 68,
    69, 80, 103, 104, 105, 112
Entitlement, 102–4, 110
Entrepreneurs, 32, 72, 81
Entry of immigrants, 11, 18–19, 27, 60
Ethnic enclaves, 66, 73, 74
Ethnic identity, 28, 64–67, 105; and
    civil rights, 69–71; and economic
    status, 67–69
Ethnic relations, 28, 69
Europe, 59; emigration from, 9–10, 24,
    27, 32, 41–42, 48; employment in,
    86; migration within, 3
European Americans, 21, 28, 75. See
    also Irish Americans
European immigrants, 74, 75; differ-
    ences in, 24; ethnic identity, 65. See
    also Irish immigrants
Exclusion of immigrants, 9, 12, 26, 27
Exemptions for immigrants, 12, 13, 17,
    48, 89
Explosion of migration flow, 11, 44–45,
    49–50, 53; prevention of, 54–58, 60;
    risk of, 18, 45–46, 59

Family, 33, 38
Family-based immigration, 17, 31, 37, 54
Family networks. See Networks
Family reunification policies, 16, 43,
    50, 53, 58, 107, 110
Federalism, 95–96, 97–98
First immigration wave, 21, 22, 24,
    25, 26
Florida, 45, 59, 95, 97, 103
Ford administration, 87
Former Soviet Union: emigration
    from, 3, 15
Freedom of movement, 60

Garment industry, 89–90

Glazer, Nathan, 64

Government: attitudes toward, 68, costs of enforcement by, 89–92; role in immigration, 93–94

Government assistance, 68, 94, 101, 103; attitudes toward, 80; claims of immigrants on, 17, 94–99, 107–12; for immigrants, 58, 59, 93, 105–6

Grasmuck, Sherri, 40

Great Depression, 27, 75, 94

Haiti, 15, 56–57

Haitian immigrants, 15, 57

Hayes-Bautista, David, 80–81

Health care, 94, 95, 99, 101, 111

Hendricks, Glenn, 37

Higham, John, 21, 24, 26

Hispanic Americans. See Latino Americans

Hispanic immigrants. See Latino immigrants

Hispanic Population in the United States, The (Bean and Tienda), 67–68

Honduran immigrants, 32

Household networks. See Networks

Human behavior, 5

Human rights, 60

Illegal immigration, 13–14, 18, 83–84; from Caribbean, 6; from Ireland, 41; from Latin America, 23; from Mexico, 33, 47, 49, 51

Immigrant (term), 24–25

Immigrant enclaves. See Ethnic enclaves

Immigrants, 27–28, 31; characteristics, 35, 80; employment, 13, 37, 48–49, 77, 81, 87–92; motivation, 32, 33–34, 35–36, 37, 38, 40, 95; political power of, 25–26, 68–69, 74,

103; population, 4, 23, 24, 27, 42; services for, 94–99, 102–6, 108–12; socioeconomic status, 27, 35, 67–69, 73, 74, 75–76, 77–80, 81–82

Immigration, 8; categories, 16; cost-benefit analysis, 19, 97–98, 104, 105–6; costs, 85, 90, 92, 93–97, 102; levels of, 9–12; limiting, 9, 17, 19; risks from, 12; waves of, 21–22, 23, 24, 25, 26, 27, 74, 75, 94, 108. See also Emigration; Illegal immigration; Legal immigration; Migration

Immigration Act (1965), 10

Immigration Act (1990), 16–17

Immigration contract, 96, 106–8, 110

Immigration laws, 41, 48, 97, 110; effects of, 9–10, 50; intent of, 16–17, 89; problems with, 13–14

Immigration policy, 93; attitudes toward, 68; changes proposed, 60, 101–2, 109–13; goals, 12, 18–19, 91, 95; problems with, 12–16, 92

Immigration Reform and Control Act (1986), 13–14, 45, 50, 87–92, 96

India, 32

Informal economy, 86

Integration of immigrants, 11–12, 18–19, 60, 86, 97, 101–2. See also Assimilation

Internal Revenue Service, 88

Investors, 16–17, 32

Ireland, 43, 44

Irish, 74

Irish Americans: influence of, 41

Irish immigrants, 32, 40, 43–44, 45, 74; motivation, 41–42, 44

Jamaica, 32

Jobs. See Employment

Johnson, Albert, 9

Kinship networks. *See* Networks

Korean-owned businesses, 72

Korean immigrants, 32, 43

Labor costs, 86, 89, 90, 92

Labor demand, 43–44, 73, 87, 90, 92, 108

Labor force, 7, 51, 76–77, 81–82, 85, 88, 90–92, 105

Labor supply, 48, 73, 92

Language: and immigrants, 22, 28, 68, 69, 80, 102–4, 105

Latin America: emigration from, 4, 6, 16, 21, 23, 32, 43. *See also* Caribbean region; Central America

Latino Americans, 27, 28, 69; attitudes of, 66, 68, 80; influence of, 6, 87, 104–5; population, 6–7, 82

Latino children, 28, 64, 74–75, 83, 105

Latino immigrants, 27, 64, 108, 112; attitudes toward, 68; characteristics, 80; differences in, 65–66, 68; economic status of, 67–69, 73, 75, 77–80, 85–86; employment, 7, 76, 87; ethnic identity, 65–70; and American culture, 25–26, 43, 67, 68, 72; residence, 66

Latino National Political Survey, 66

Latino-owned businesses, 71, 72, 73, 81

"Latino Voices," 68

Lau v. Nichols (Supreme Court decision), 103

Lazarus, Emma, 31

Legal immigration, 10, 16–19, 22, 31; from Asia, 24; from Central America, 53; from Mexico, 23, 50

Linkages: in migration, 5–6, 33, 36–37, 38, 43, 45, 46, 47–49. *See also* Networks

Living standards, 37–38. *See also* Poverty

Local government, 59, 94–99

Los Angeles (Calif.), 48, 97; economy, 49, 77–78; riots (1992), 71–72; social conditions, 80–81

Low-skilled jobs, 49, 76

Low-wage labor, 7, 14, 43–44, 73, 77–80, 83, 85–86, 87–92, 112–13

Manufacturing sector, 22, 49, 77, 49, 89–90

Mariel boatlift (Cuba), 45, 96

McCarran-Walter Act, 48

Meissner, Doris, 59–60

Melting pot model, 64, 65, 66, 67

Mexican Americans: economic status, 83; residence, 25, 48

Mexican immigrants, 32, 39–40, 46, 50–51; characteristics, 33, 35, 36–37; economic status, 78, 79, 80; employment, 13, 37, 48–49, 77; population, 23, 24, 27, 42, 49, 50

Mexico, 39–40, 47, 48, 49–50, 51; migration within, 35; relations with United States, 54–56

Miami (Fla.), 25–26, 69

Middle class, 7, 32, 73, 75, 83

Migrant labor, 13, 21, 33, 48

Migrants. *See* Immigrants

Migration, 3–5, 6. *See also* Emigration; Immigration

Migration patterns, 33, 34, 36–37, 42, 46, 50, 108

Migration stages, 42–46

Minimum wage, 77, 86

Minority groups, 27–28, 102, 112; *See also* Blacks; Irish Americans; Latino Americans; Mexican Americans

Mobility of Labor and Capital, The (Sassen), 42

Moral judgments: about immigrants, 9, 12, 15–16, 97

Mosaic model, 64, 65, 66

Moynihan, Daniel P., 64
Multiculturalism, 18, 64, 67

NAFTA. *See* North American Free
Trade Agreement
National identity, 65; American, 7,
26–27; Latino, 66. *See also* Ethnic
identity
National interest: and immigration, 12,
19, 57, 93, 101
Nationalism, 76
National Origins Act (1924), 9, 10, 16, 48
Native Americans, 27
Networks, 73, 80, 81; and emigration,
35–37, 38, 40, 54, 107
New York City, 27, 37, 69; conditions
in, 25, 76–77; riots (1992), 72–73
New York State, 95
Nicaragua, 14, 57
Nicaraguan immigrants, 14, 43
North American Free Trade Agreement
(NAFTA), 54, 55
Norway, 32

Paine, Thomas, 26
Panama, 32
Pessar, Patricia R., 40
Philippine immigrants, 24, 32, 43
Political refugees, 15
Politics: and immigration, 9, 41, 45,
48–49, 87–88
Portes, Alejandro, 83
Postindustrial economy, 22, 76
Population, 4–5, 10, 24, 42, 75, 82
Poverty, 50, 73, 76, 77–80, 81, 83, 107;
costs of, 74–75; and emigration,
32–33, 36; and ethnic identity, 67–68
Poverty wages. *See* Low-wage labor
Puerto Ricans, 25, 27
Push-pull model, 33–34

Quota system, 9, 10, 16, 48

Racial differences, 18, 27
Railroads, 48
Reagan, Ronald, 45
Reagan administration, 87, 89
Redwood City (Calif.), 77
Refugees, 14–16, 57, 93, 96, 107; defini-
tion, 15
Relative deprivation theory, 37–38
Religion: and immigrants, 22, 74
Remittances, 5, 36, 38–40, 51, 55
Revueltas, Art, 74–75
Right to stay (principle), 60
Rivera Center. *See* Tomás Rivera Center
Rouse, Roger, 77

Safety value model, 33–34
Salvadoran immigrants, 14, 15, 53, 73;
economic status, 78, 79, 80
Sassen, Saskia, 42, 43–44, 76–77, 81
Second immigration wave, 21, 22, 24,
25, 26, 27, 74, 75
Service sector, 76–77, 90–91
Skilled labor, 16–17, 32, 35
Social change, 4–5, 11, 17, 26–27, 70,
107
Social justice, 86, 87, 104
Social welfare, 68, 80, 94–99, 101–2,
108–12
Southwest, 48, 69, 75; economy, 13, 87;
population, 25
Special categories of immigrants, 12
Statue of Liberty, 31
Sweden, 32

Taiwanese immigrants, 32
Taxes: for immigrants (proposed),
110–11; paid by immigrants, 96, 97
Texas, 66, 95
Texas Proviso (1952), 48
Third immigration wave, 21, 22, 23, 27,
94, 108
Tienda, Marta, 67–68

Tomás Rivera Center, 72, 77
Transplanted, The (Bodner), 32
Travel costs (in immigration), 36

Undocumented immigrants. *See* Illegal
   immigrants
United States: economy, 22, 48, 75–76,
   85–86, 90–92; foreign policy, 15, 18,
   54, 56–57, 58, 60; history, 21, 24,
   47–48, 94; as nation of immigrants,
   5, 21–22; social conditions, 17,
   26–27, 70, 107
Upward mobility, 7, 66, 73, 74, 75–76,
   82, 83, 85–86, 89, 92
Urban development, 22, 74
Urban underclass, 7, 19, 28, 74–75
Urban violence, 71–73, 112

Venezuela, 45
Vietnam War, 49
Vietnamese immigrants, 15, 43
Visits to United States, 25, 36

Wages, 33, 76, 91. *See also* Low-wage
   labor; Minimum wage
Welfare recipients, 80
Wilson, Pete, 94, 96, 99, 106
Women: employment, 76, 90
Women immigrants, 40
Work force. *See* Labor force
Working class, 75, 76, 78–82, 85–86
Working poor, 77–78, 80, 81, 82, 83.
   See also Low-wage labor
World War II, 9, 27, 48, 75–76

About the Author

R oberto Suro was born and raised in Washington, D.C., the son of Hispanic immigrants. After graduating from Yale (B.A. 1973) and Columbia (M.S. Journalism 1974), he began a career as a newspaper reporter in Chicago. In 1978 he became a correspondent for *Time* magazine, eventually doing tours in its Chicago, Washington, Beirut, and Rome bureaus. From 1985 to 1993 he worked as bureau chief for the *New York Times*, first in Rome and then in Houston. In March 1994 he became a staff writer for the *Washington Post*. Suro is currently completing a book on Latino immigration due to be published in 1995 by Alfred A. Knopf .